EDDIE CAMPBELL

His Domestic Apocalypse:

THE FATE OF
THE ARTIST

An Autobiographical Novel,

with Typographical Anomalies,

in which the Author

DOES NOT APPEAR

as Himself.

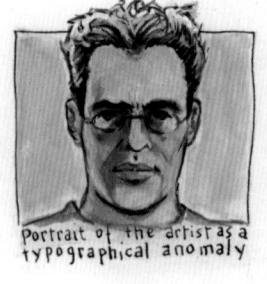

Portrait of the artist as a
typographical anomaly

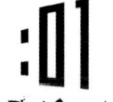

First Second
New York & London

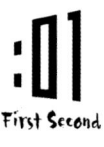

First Second

Published by First Second
First Second is an imprint of Roaring Brook Press, a division of
Holtzbrinck Publishing Holdings Limited Partnership
175 Fifth Avenue, New York, NY 10010

Distributed in Canada by H. B. Fenn and Company Ltd.
Distributed in the United Kingdom by Macmillan Children's
Books, a division of Pan Macmillan.

Jacket design by Charles Orr.

Thanks to Michael Evans Designs, for the use of facilities.

Photographing and being photographed by Hayley Campbell.

Thanks to Matt Bell for telling me a couple of anecdotes on the subject of studying acting,
and Todd DeZago, Dan Best and Daren White for reading and spotting problems.

Cataloging-in-Publication Data is on file at the Library of Congress.

ISBN-13: 978-1-59643-133-1 (paperback)
ISBN-10: 1-59643-133-4 (paperback)

COLLECTOR'S EDITION
ISBN-13: 978-1-59643-171-3
ISBN-10: 1-59643-171-7

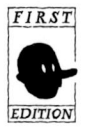

FIRST

EDITION

First Second books are available for special promotions and premiums.
For details, contact: Director of Special Markets, Holtzbrinck Publishers.

First Edition April 2006

Printed in China

10 9 8 7 6 5 4 3 2 1

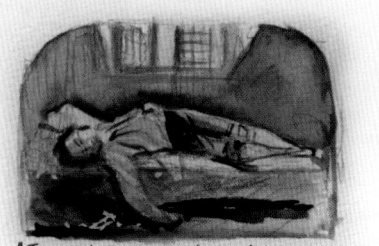

"The poet Chatterton (1752-70), lying dead
in his Holborn garret, self-slain beside the
creations of his disordered genius, torn up
by his own hand."

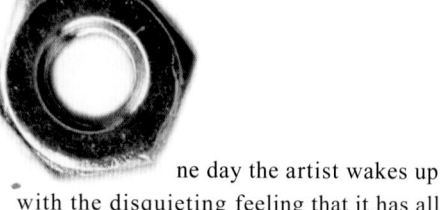

ne day the artist wakes up
with the disquieting feeling that it has all
gone
wr o n g .

The man in the street supposes the problem
to be something called 'writer's block.' In
fact the artist has come to despise **his art**
    his **self**
        and his **readers**.

It is difficult to obtain sympathy for this
condition.

You
    can
    all
        go
        to
        fuck   zzzzz

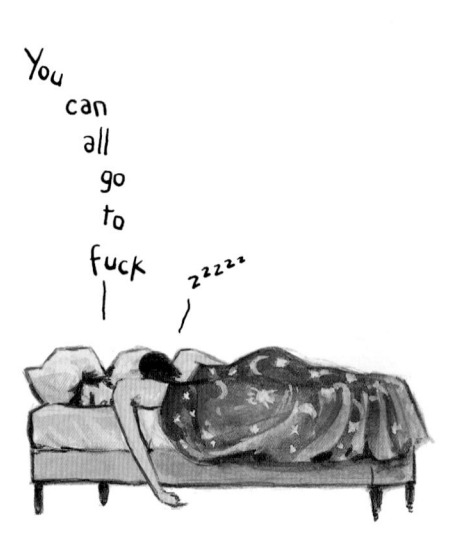

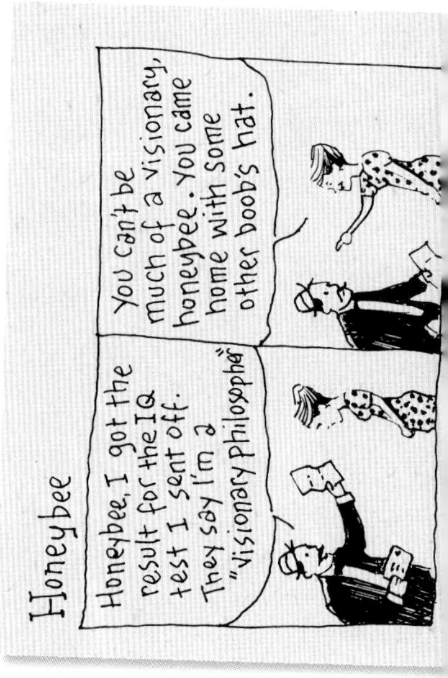
Honeybee
Honeybee, I got the result for the IQ test I sent off. They say I'm a "visionary philosopher"
You can't be much of a visionary, honeybee. You came home with some other boob's hat.

Part the First

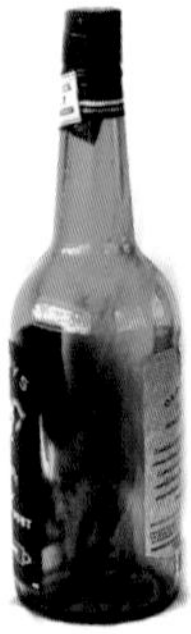

n the beginning there was just the picture. Found on the floor of the rented storage locker.

"If any words came with it, they're not there now. They've shifted." the daughter says, obviously paraphrasing something.

"Most people would leave a note."

"Yes, well, he left a picture."

"You say he made his living as an artist? I only ask because it's not much of a picture."

"What are you: a detective or a critic?"

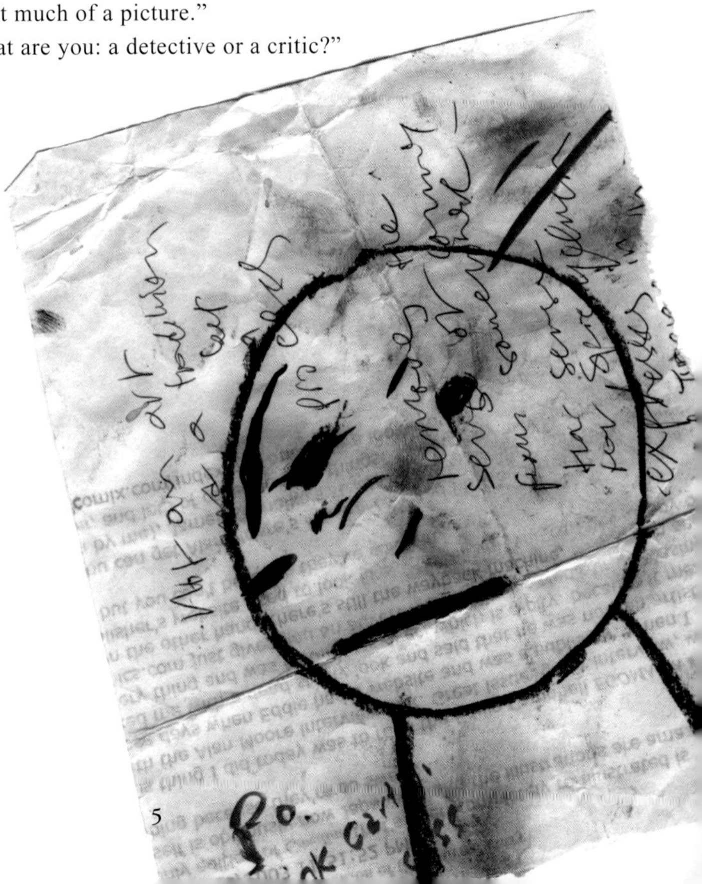

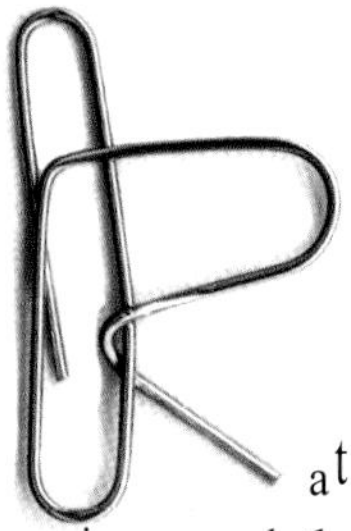

attle, rattttle, goes the door around its rollers and again around the rafters of the Ashgrove self-storage depot.

I step in.

Everything is bagged in black plastic, logically labeled, and neatly shelved.

"He was the original Seymour," offers the daughter, perhaps a reference to the character in the movie, *Ghost World*. Oh, to be a writer and create a character that gives a permanent name to a type like that; a Svengali

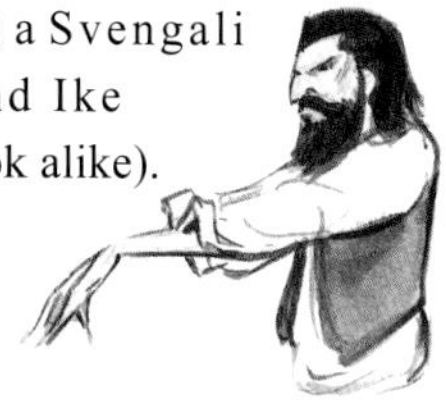

, a Lolita,

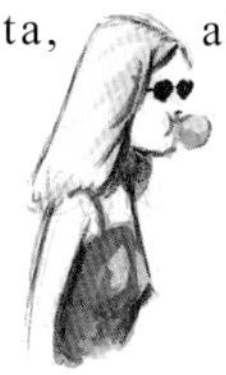

a Mrs. Malaprop,

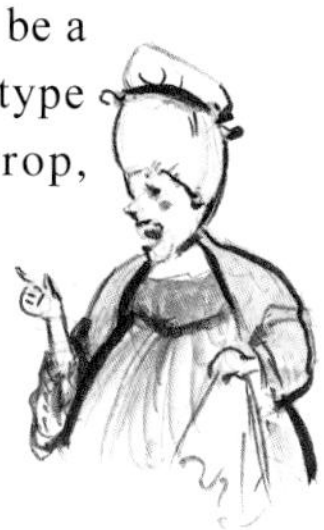

Mike and Ike (they look alike).

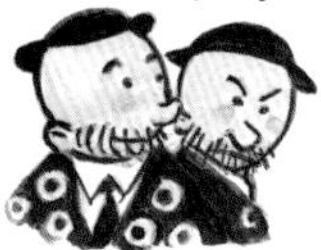
(after Goldberg)

The wife is parking the car. I use her momentary absence to inquire about 'the state of marriage in modern times.' "Did he go out for a six-pack and not come back?"

"Who knows? He was always in the shit with Mum. It's just the depth that varied. He left home once before; packed shirts and toiletries in his backpack and headed off on his bike. He was back in time to walk Monty at four."

"Most people leave home for longer than that five times a week."

"So now you're a comedian."

There isn't a stray Post-it note to give a clue to whatever new autobiographical ramble Eddie Campbell might have been working on the day he went missing. The wife is vague. "*How to be an ArtiSt*," she suggests, with the Australian habit of raising the voice on the last syllable, unintentionally turning the title into a question (who would want to be one?).

"He became obsessed with all kinds of obscure artists, or composers, or whatever, like Johann Schobert."

"You mean *Franz* Schubert?"

"I'm sure it was Schobert."

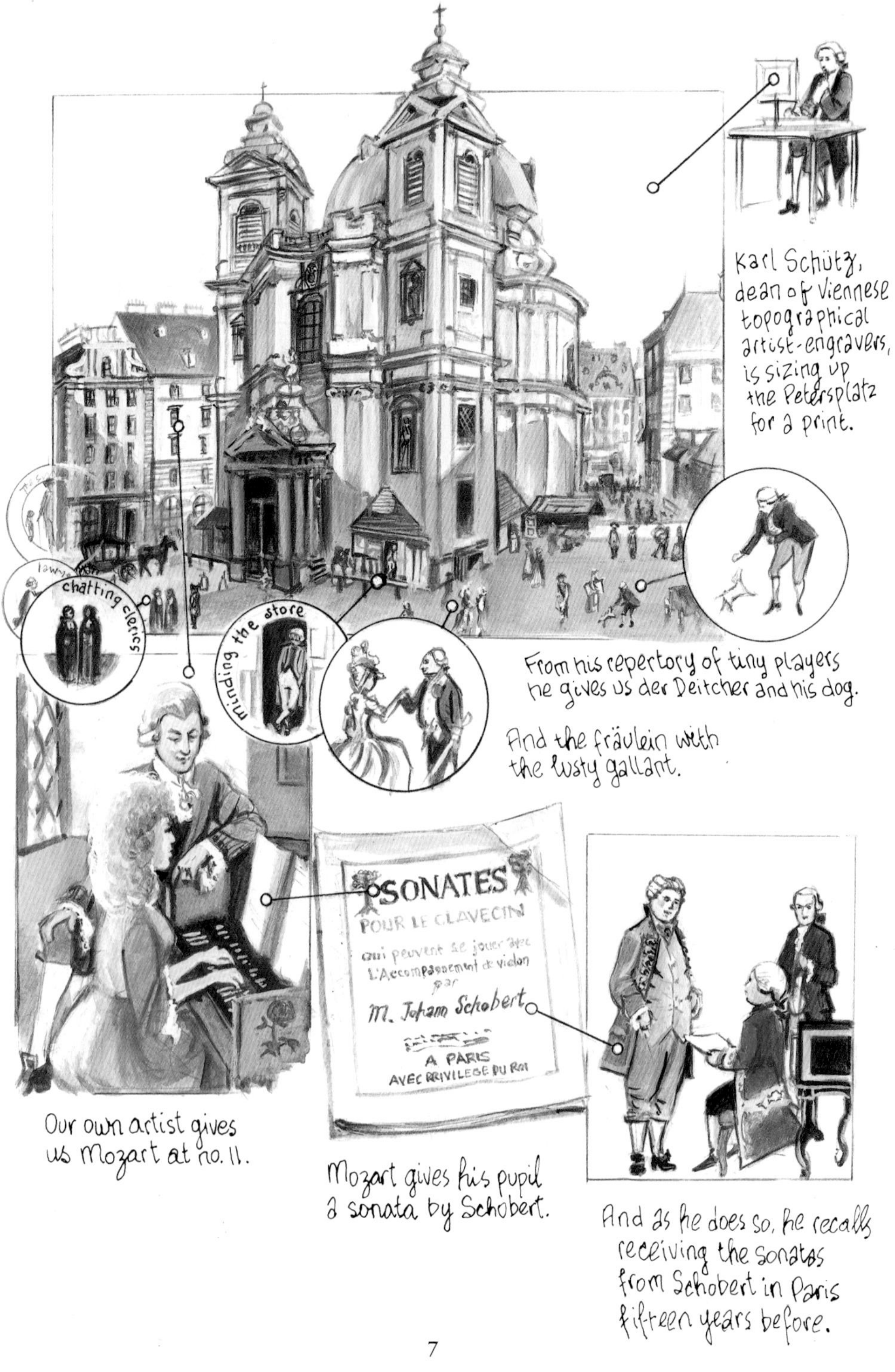
Karl Schütz, dean of Viennese topographical artist-engravers, is sizing up the Petersplatz for a print.
chatting clerics
minding the store
From his repertory of tiny players he gives us der Deitcher and his dog.
And the fräulein with the lusty gallant.
Our own artist gives us Mozart at no. 11.
SONATES
POUR LE CLAVECIN
qui peuvent se jouer avec
L'Accompagnement de violon
par
M. Joham Schobert
A PARIS
AVEC PRIVILEGE DU ROI
Mozart gives his pupil a sonata by Schobert.
And as he does so, he recalls receiving the sonatas from Schobert in Paris fifteen years before.

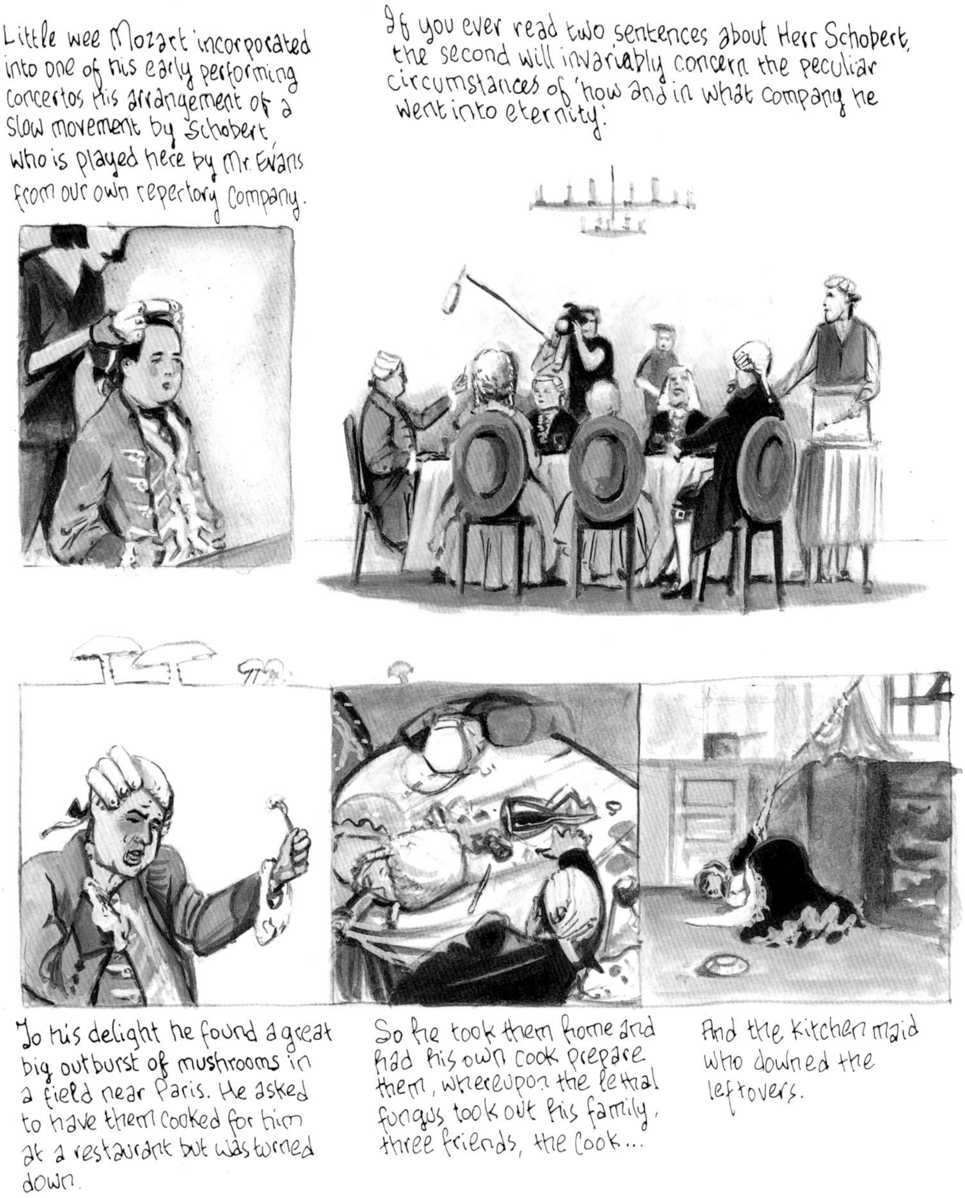
Little wee Mozart incorporated into one of his early performing concertos his arrangement of a slow movement by Schobert, who is played here by Mr. Evans from our own repertory company.
If you ever read two sentences about Herr Schobert, the second will invariably concern the peculiar circumstances of 'how and in what company he went into eternity.
To his delight he found a great big outburst of mushrooms in a field near Paris. He asked to have them cooked for him at a restaurant but was turned down.
So he took them home and had his own cook prepare them, whereupon the lethal fungus took out his family, three friends, the cook...
And the kitchen maid who downed the leftovers.

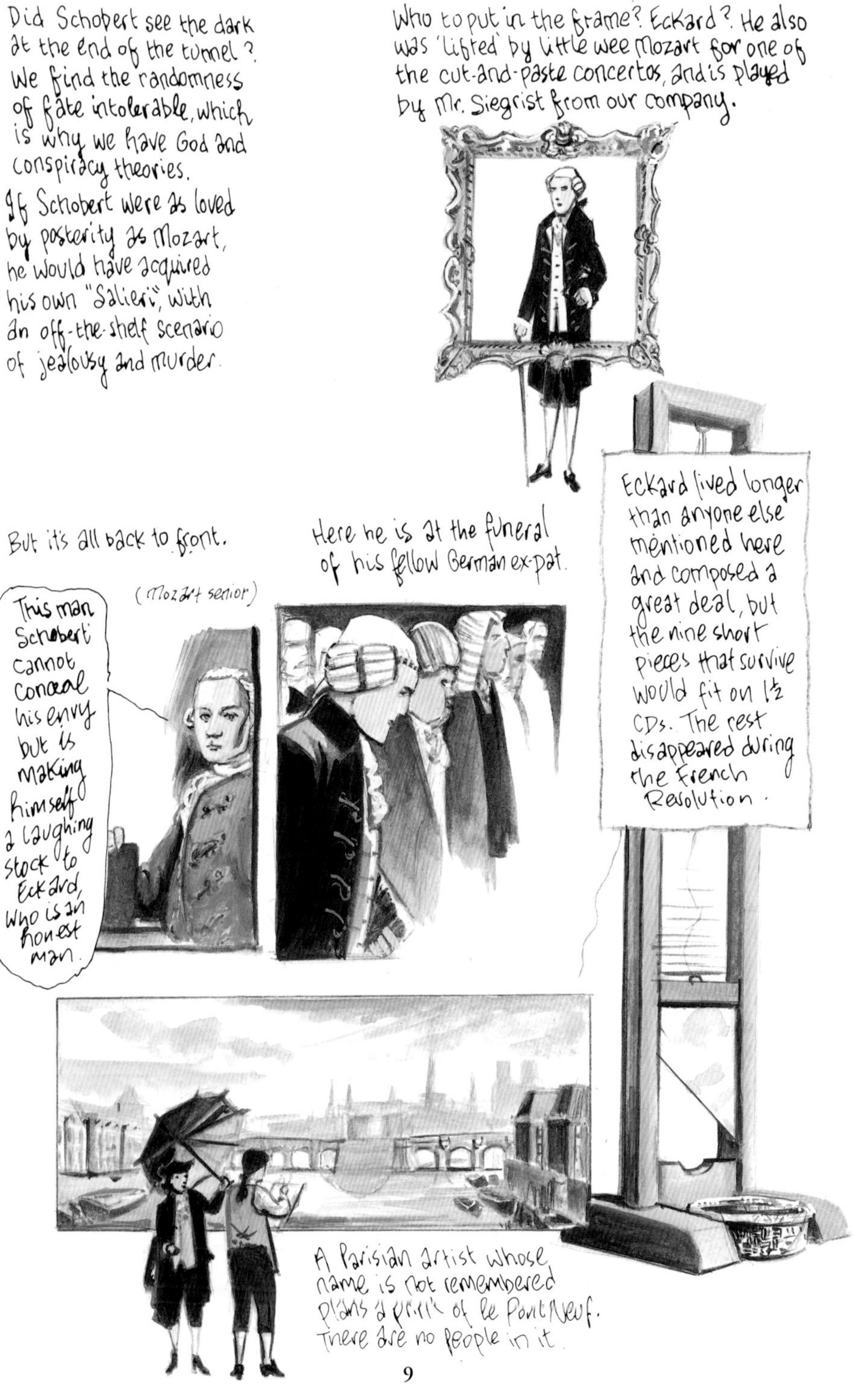
Did Schobert see the dark at the end of the tunnel? We find the randomness of fate intolerable, which is why we have God and conspiracy theories.
If Schobert were as loved by posterity as Mozart, he would have acquired his own "Salieri", with an off-the-shelf scenario of jealousy and murder.
Who to put in the frame? Eckard? He also was 'lifted' by little wee Mozart for one of the cut-and-paste concertos, and is played by Mr. Siegrist from our company.
But it's all back to front.
(Mozart senior)
This man Schobert cannot conceal his envy but is making himself a laughing stock to Eckard, who is an honest man.
Here he is at the funeral of his fellow German ex-pat.
Eckard lived longer than anyone else mentioned here and composed a great deal, but the nine short pieces that survive would fit on 1½ CDs. The rest disappeared during the French Revolution.
A Parisian artist whose name is not remembered plans a print of le Pont Neuf. There are no people in it.

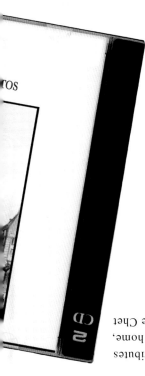

Eddie Campbell

"Are these discs that he burned for himself?"

"I don't think he ever figured out how to do that. Wait, are you looking at the hand-lettering?" asks the daughter, who has evidently made a typological study of the 'Seymour.'

"The proper printed spines were never good enough for Dad. He'd always put in his own on a strip of white paper, neatly hand-lettered with composer and date and some tiny hieroglyphs. You'll have to ask him about it yourself when you find him. But, of course, by then you won't be interested any more.

"So he'd crack the clear plastic case apart and slip it in. He wanted to survey the entire history of music, in chronological order it goes without saying, while sipping his after-dinner port from his throne at the end of the table."

"I can't help noticing that the booklets are all upside down."

"That's just his solution to the design fault of the CD case. You can never get the booklet in and out without wrecking it. You must admit it's pretty lame. So he'd keep them his own way. All two thousand, or however many there are, of the CDs on those shelves, have their booklets in upside down. Technically it's the case that's upside down. You just have to get used to opening it from the left, and he'd be pissed off to see you leaving the pictures upside down like that. Make sure you flip the cases before he gets home."

"When he'd go abroad for a convention," contributes the wife, encouraged by the hint that he might be on his way home, "I used to ask him to leave out some of my favorites, like Chet"

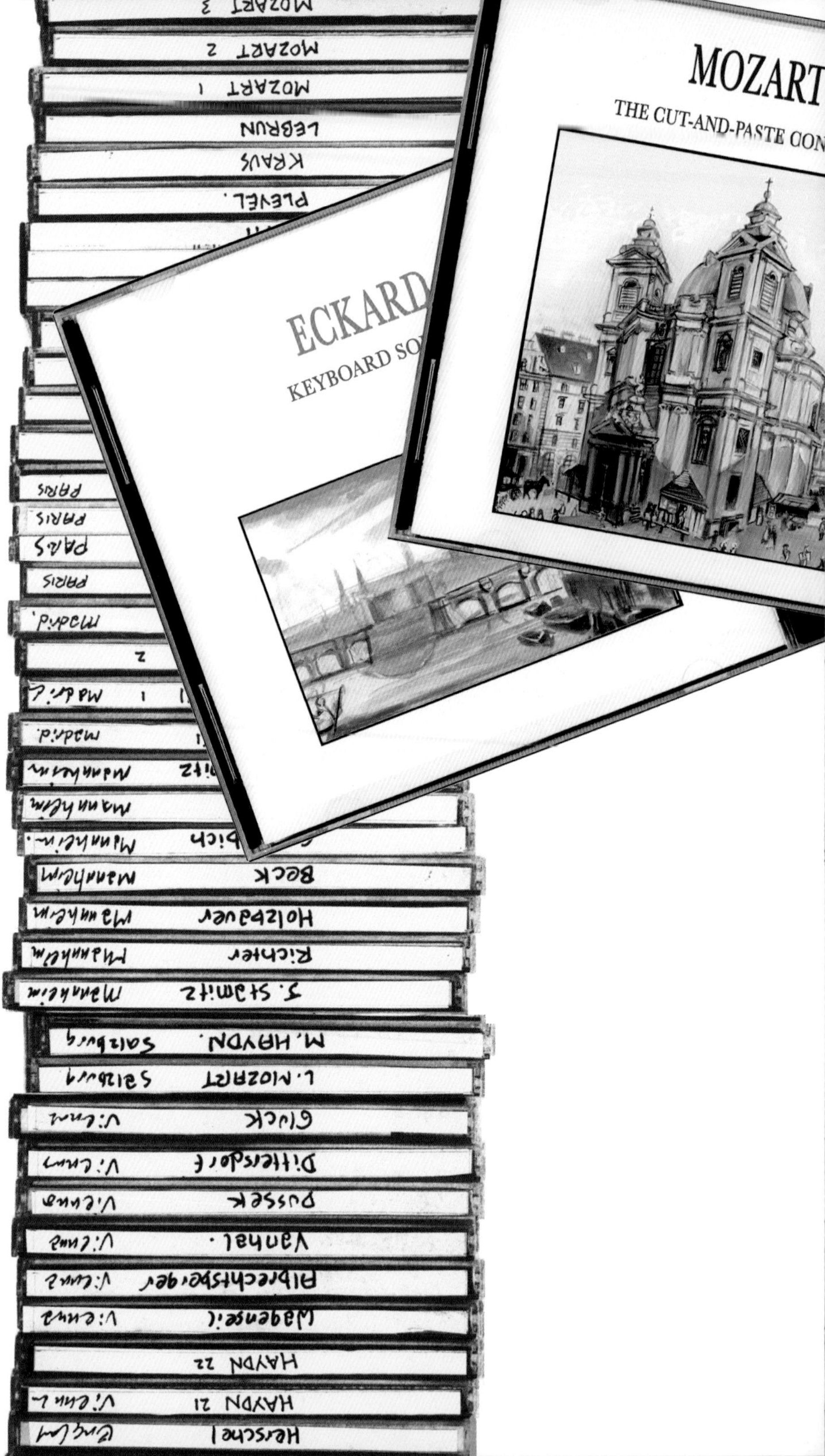
MOZART

Baker or some monks chanting, but I stopped because I could picture him lying awake at night in Madrid or London fretting about them being left out of sequence."

"It's like the actual history of music, art, and everything would fall apart in his absence, as though he were the one in charge of keeping an eye on it," observes the daughter insightfully.

"Eventually he had far too many CDs for the shelf so he'd buy those hinged insert frames for two-in-one cases. Then he doubled up every CD in his collection until he had condensed the whole lot into half its space. Of course, since he was also buying new CDs at the same rate it always looked like the same volume of stuff. I think he felt guilty about the money he was spending, even though he scoured secondhand shops and got most of it half-price. In his head he was probably still fifteen and nicking his school lunch money."

"If you ask me," offers the wife, "he might as well be somewhere else, because he always was in his head anyway ... Vienna ... Paris ... Athens. He couldn't drink a glass of sherry without making a leisurely visit, all in his head, to whatever part of Spain it is where they make it. In fact, he insisted that if a wine didn't agreeably escort you somewhere, then you might as well drink water. He tried doing that too when he was saving money, but he'd always end up gulping too fast and choking himself."

"As Cal said, you'd be talking to him when he was miles away and if he occasionally opened his mouth you'd know he'd heard one of your words. Hey, Cal, remember the time you mooched two dollars off Dad to buy a condom?"

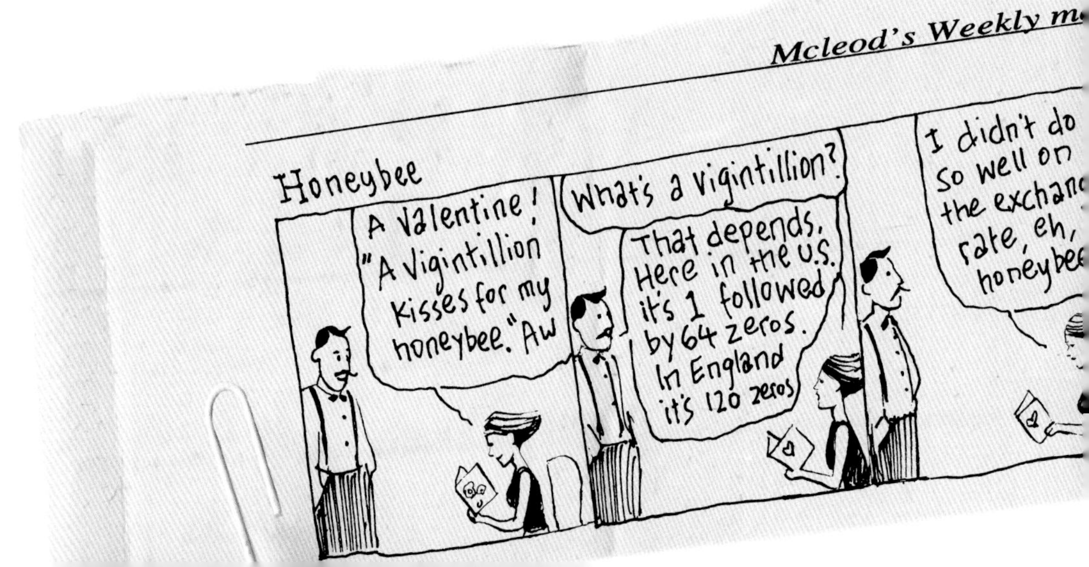
Mcleod's Weekly m
Honeybee
A Valentine! "A Vigintillion Kisses for my honeybee." Aw
What's a vigintillion?
That depends. Here in the U.S. it's 1 followed by 64 zeros. In England it's 120 zeros
I didn't do so well on the exchan rate, eh, honeybe

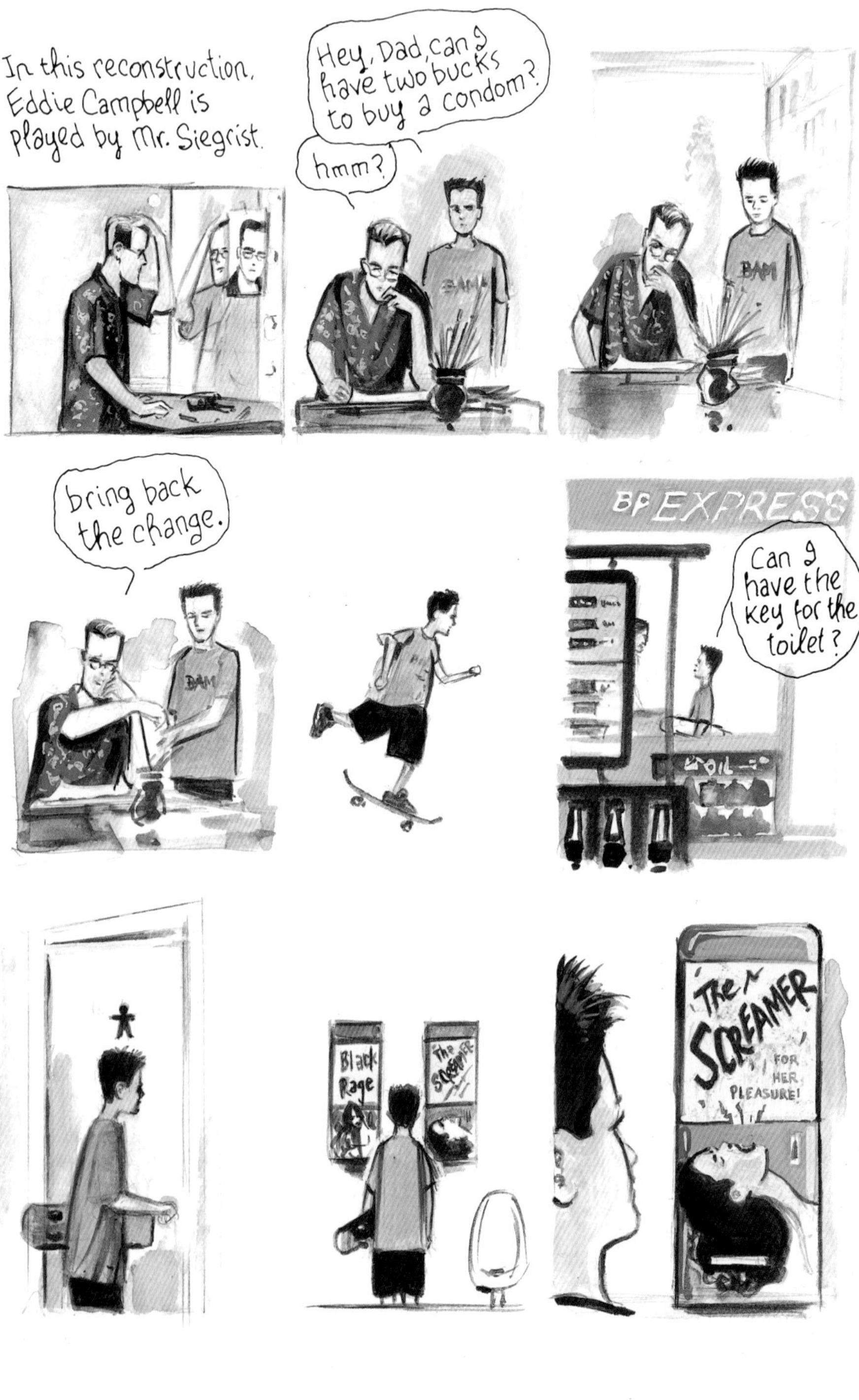
In this reconstruction, Eddie Campbell is played by Mr. Siegrist.
Hey, Dad, can I have two bucks to buy a condom?
hmm?
BAM
bring back the change.
BP EXPRESS
Can I have the key for the toilet?
OIL
Black Rage
The SCREAMER
The SCREAMER FOR HER PLEASURE!

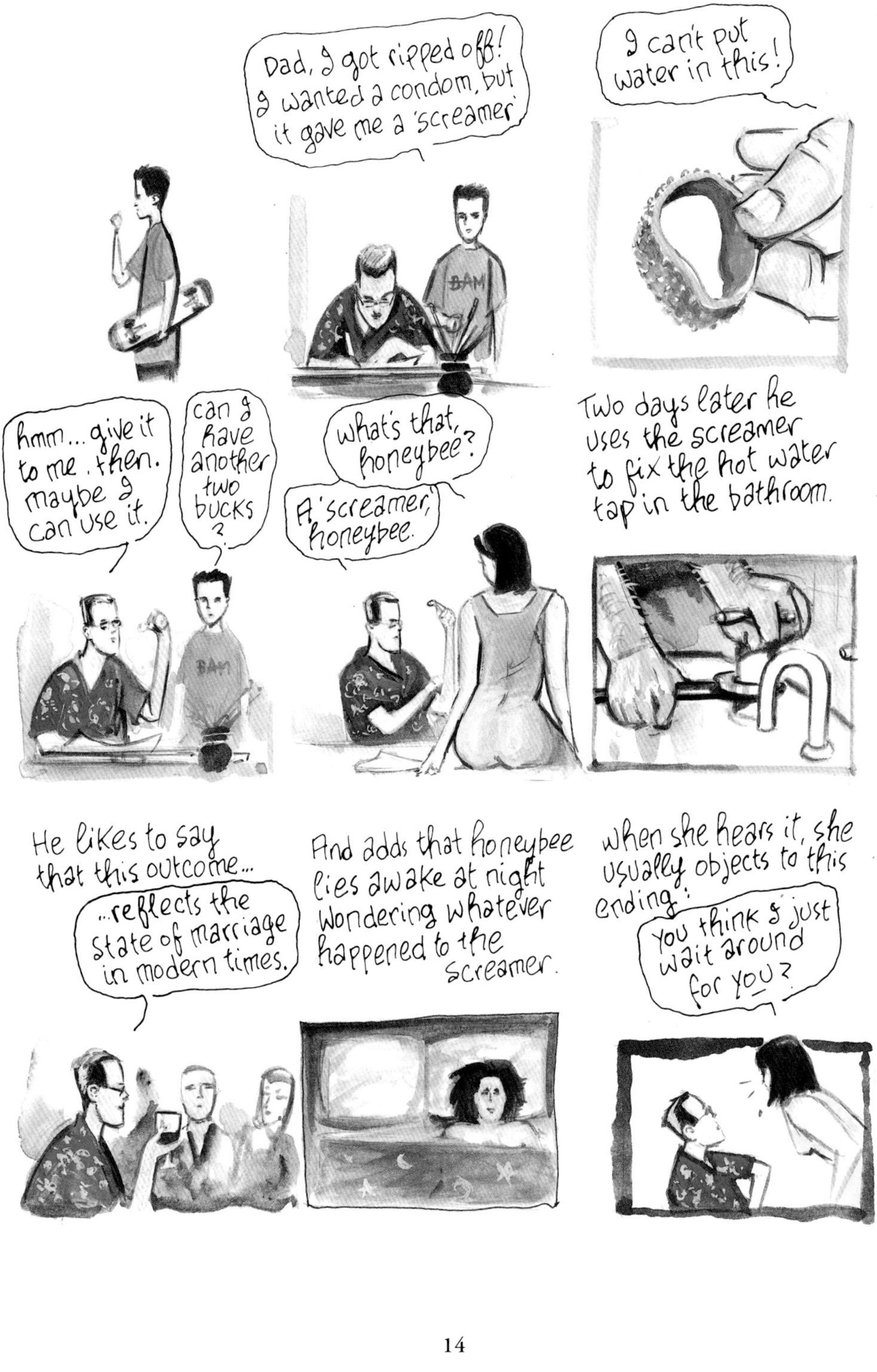
Dad, I got ripped off! I wanted a condom, but it gave me a 'screamer'
I can't put water in this!
hmm... give it to me. then. maybe I can use it.
can I have another two bucks ?
what's that, honeybee?
A 'screamer,' honeybee.
Two days later he uses the screamer to fix the hot water tap in the bathroom.
He likes to say that this outcome...
...reflects the state of marriage in modern times.
And adds that honeybee lies awake at night wondering whatever happened to the screamer.
when she hears it, she usually objects to this ending:
You think I just wait around for you?

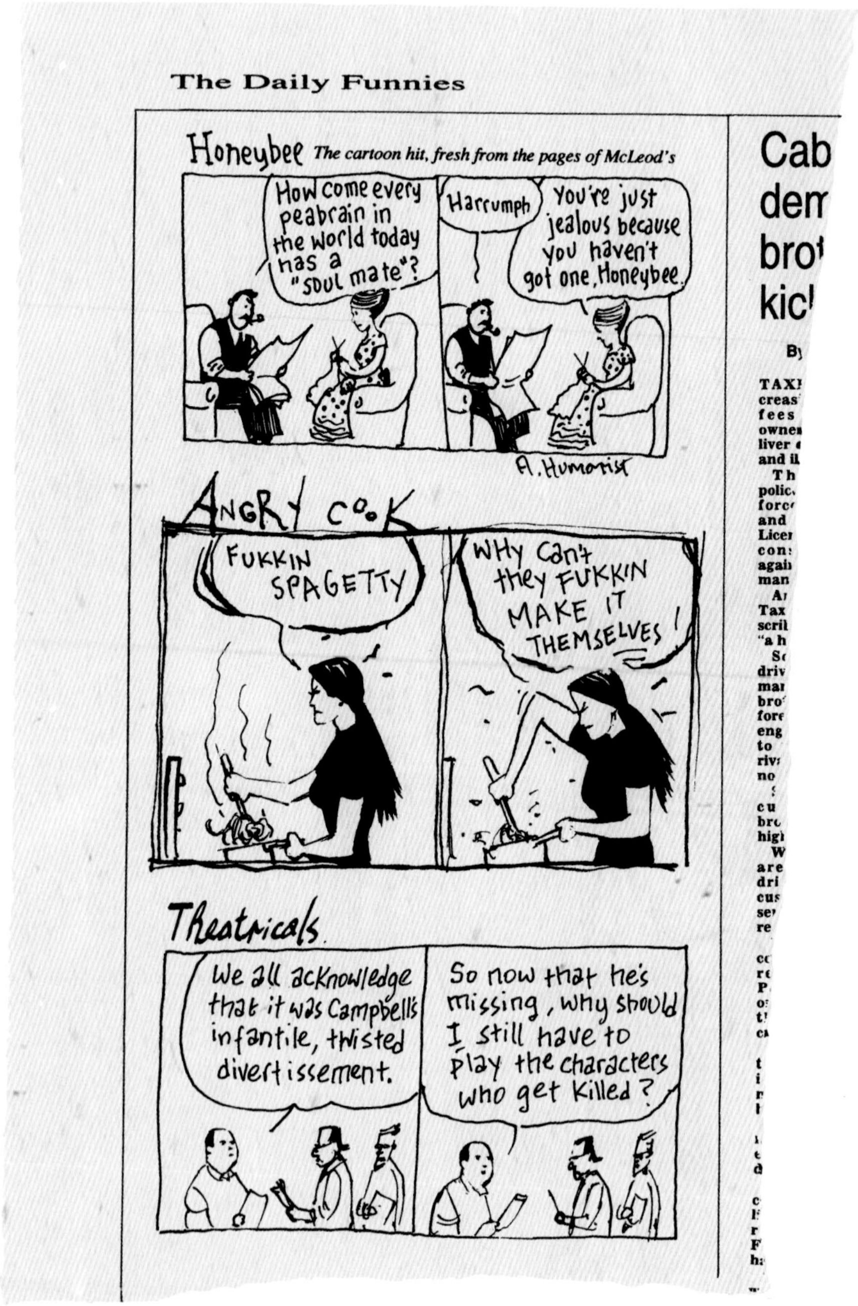
The Daily Funnies
Honeybee The cartoon hit, fresh from the pages of McLeod's
How come every peabrain in the world today has a "soul mate"?
Harrumph
You're just jealous because you haven't got one, Honeybee.
A. Humorist
ANGRY COOK
FUKKIN SPAGETTY
WHY CAN'T THEY FUKKIN MAKE IT THEMSELVES!
Theatricals
We all acknowledge that it was Campbell's infantile, twisted divertissement.
So now that he's missing, why should I still have to play the characters who get killed?

Tape Transcript. Unpublished interview.
Interviewer unidentified

INTERVIEWER: *I should have had the tape on during lunch. Maybe we can just cover some of that stuff briefly again. This is probably for the Comics Journal, so I'm hoping to get some insights into your dad's work and methods. Feel free to talk about that stuff in detail.*
(waitress appears)

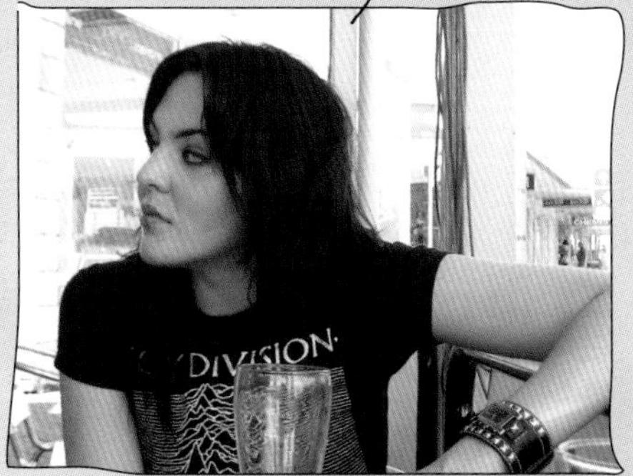

HAYLEY CAMPBELL: Ta. The beer's mine. Had to get out of that house. It's full of bloody movie people.

INTERVIEWER: *What's that all about?*

HAYLEY : It's some arty film Dad agreed to be involved with and when he buggered off it was too late to shelve the project. So we've got to go along with all this crap because of another contract he didn't read properly.

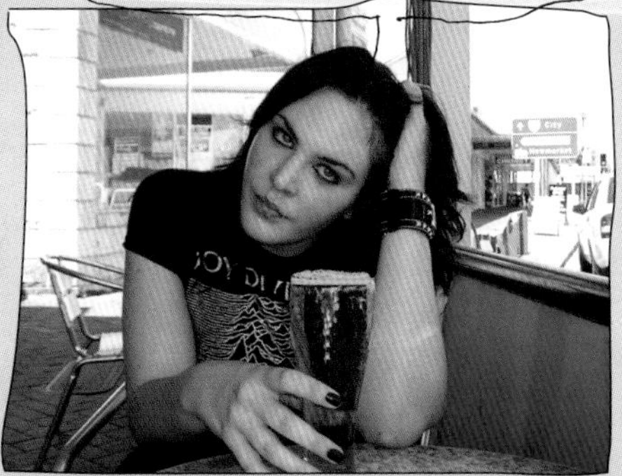

INTERVIEWER: *There's an investigation into your father's disappearance?*

HAYLEY: Yup. 'Inspector Gadget' 's looking into it. He's attaching a lot of importance to a scrap of paper he found on the floor of the locker. You can tell he's never lived with an artist. The artist puts a picture on the floor so he can accidentally stumble on it coming from different directions and see the effect as though for the first time.

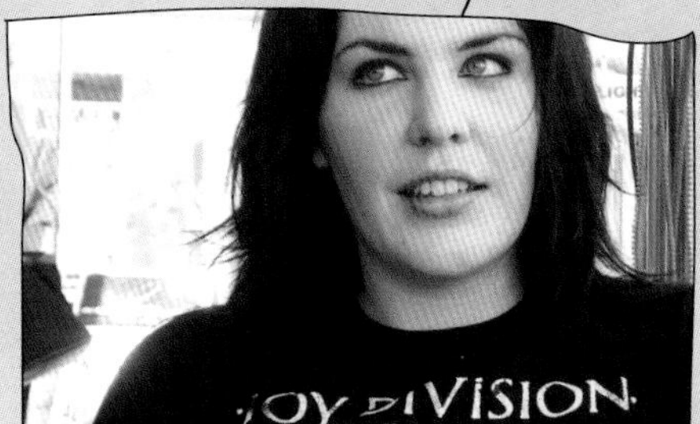
JOY DIVISION

Trouble is, everybody else stumbles on it. We're always being ambushed by pictures. When Monty was a pup he once shat all over a page. And I saw a From Hell page on eBay once with the unmistakable perforations of kitten fangs in the top corner. It's a picture of God, by the way, but we're not going to tell him that.

INTERVIEWER: *God?*

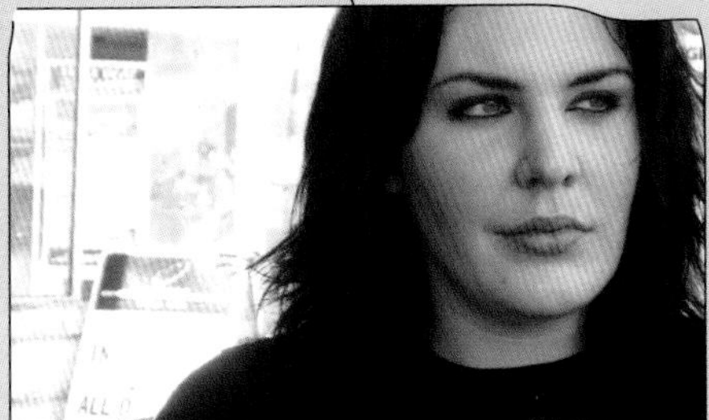

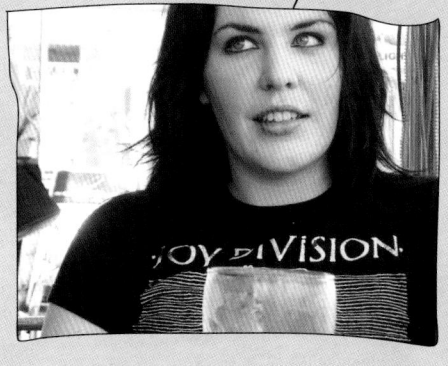

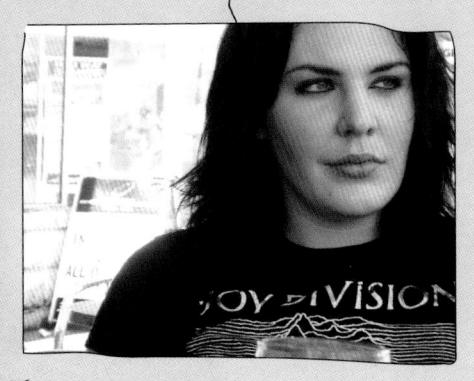

HAYLEY: Yeah, in our house God's a crayon drawing. By God I mean a sort of metaphorical god. Jeezis, you've got me talking like him now. And if anybody said 'Jeezis' he'd go 'No: Eddie Campbell. Jeezis is the one with the sandals.' He once put God in an *Eyeball Kid* story and had me draw it. To get the right effect of God being a kid's drawing. I was eight at the time.

Dad used to say that he thought God was his best creation and he liked to think the feeling was mutual. you've no idea how boring that sounds after the twentieth time.

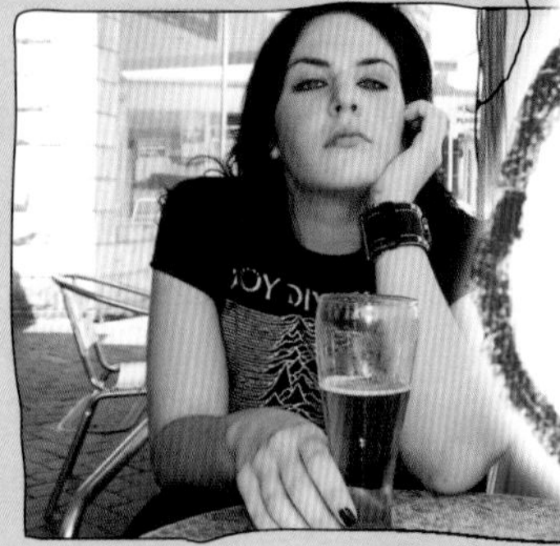

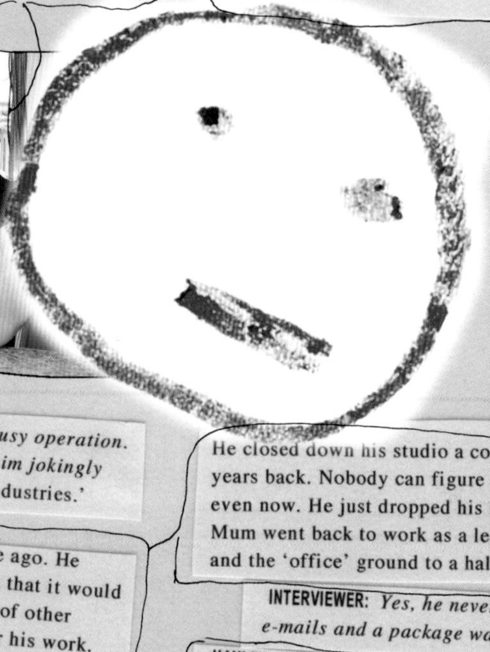

INTERVIEWER: *Your dad ran a busy operation. One person who worked for him jokingly referred to it as* 'Campbell Industries.'

HAYLEY: That was a long time ago. He had this arse-backwards idea that it would be romantic to have a patina of other people's thumbprints all over his work. But that was before he went into meltdown.

He closed down his studio a couple of years back. Nobody can figure it out even now. He just dropped his bundle. Mum went back to work as a legal typist and the 'office' ground to a halt.

INTERVIEWER: *Yes, he never answered my e-mails and a package was returned.*

HAYLEY: Well, People talk to him in the same room and never get an answer.

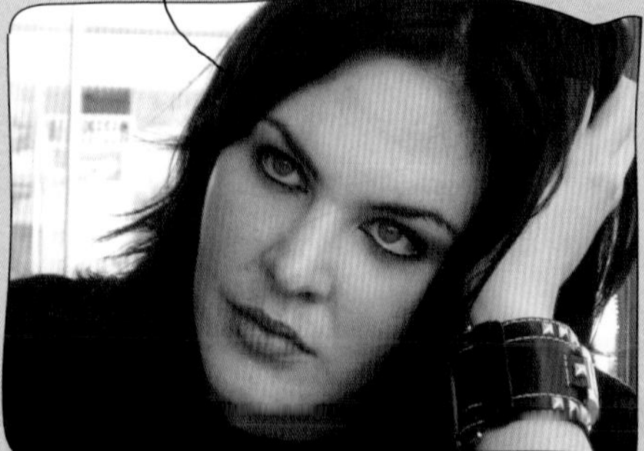

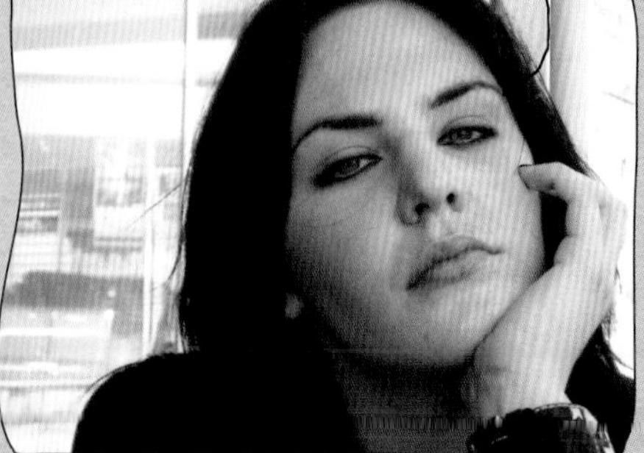

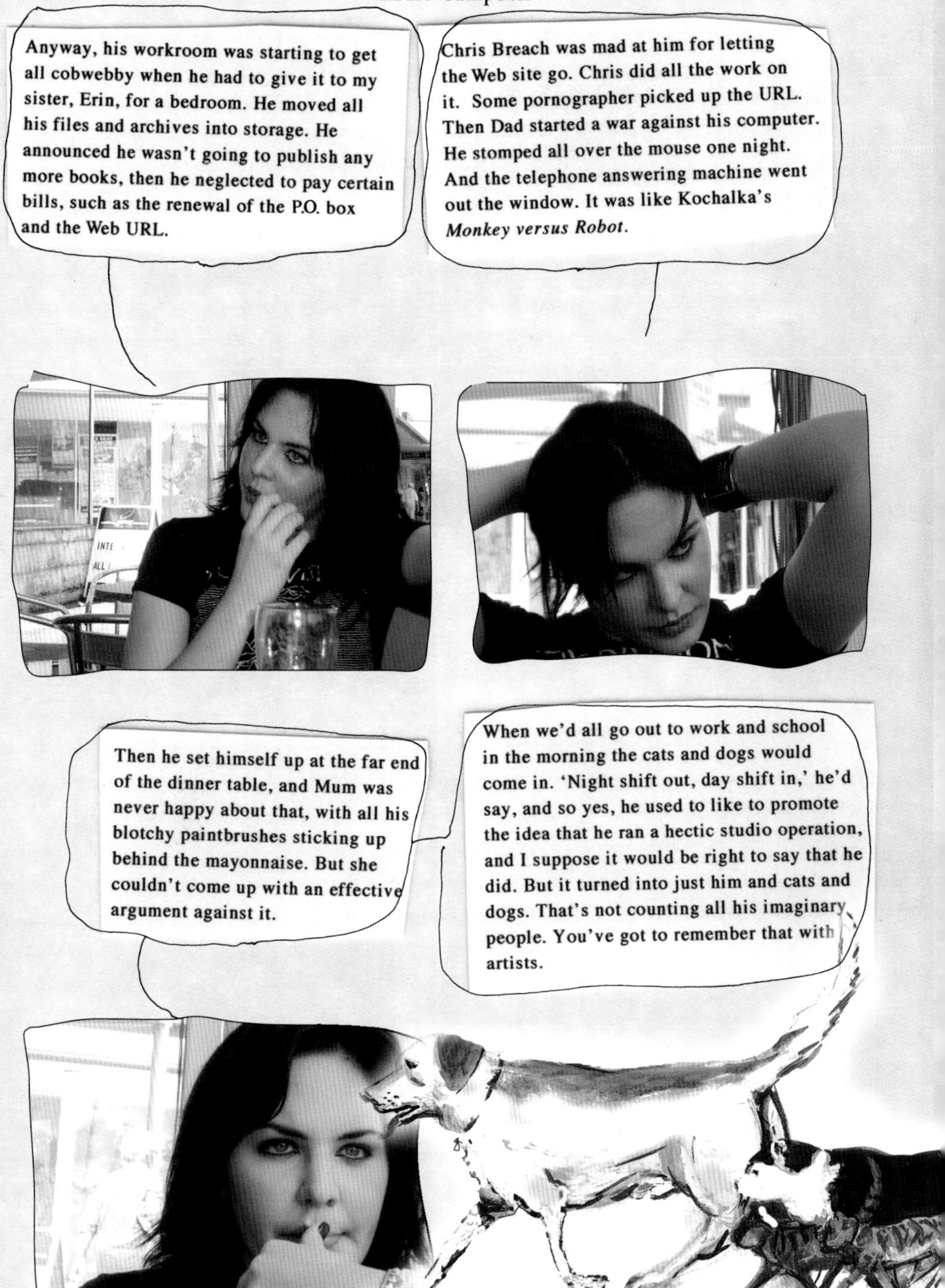
Anyway, his workroom was starting to get all cobwebby when he had to give it to my sister, Erin, for a bedroom. He moved all his files and archives into storage. He announced he wasn't going to publish any more books, then he neglected to pay certain bills, such as the renewal of the P.O. box and the Web URL.
Chris Breach was mad at him for letting the Web site go. Chris did all the work on it. Some pornographer picked up the URL. Then Dad started a war against his computer. He stomped all over the mouse one night. And the telephone answering machine went out the window. It was like Kochalka's *Monkey versus Robot*.
Then he set himself up at the far end of the dinner table, and Mum was never happy about that, with all his blotchy paintbrushes sticking up behind the mayonnaise. But she couldn't come up with an effective argument against it.
When we'd all go out to work and school in the morning the cats and dogs would come in. 'Night shift out, day shift in,' he'd say, and so yes, he used to like to promote the idea that he ran a hectic studio operation, and I suppose it would be right to say that he did. But it turned into just him and cats and dogs. That's not counting all his imaginary people. You've got to remember that with artists.
The Day shift

INTERVIEWER: *So let me get this picture right. He worked at one end of the dinner table and to eat he moved down to the other end?*

HAYLEY: Yeah, it's difficult to get anybody to listen sympathetically to your whining when your life consists of moving up and down the dinner table.

INTERVIEWER: *I'm trying to figure out his mindset. It sounds like he had nothing to complain about.*

HAYLEY: I don't think he ever did have. But he'd sit at home and get pissed off all the time. He'd seethe and simmer and boil.

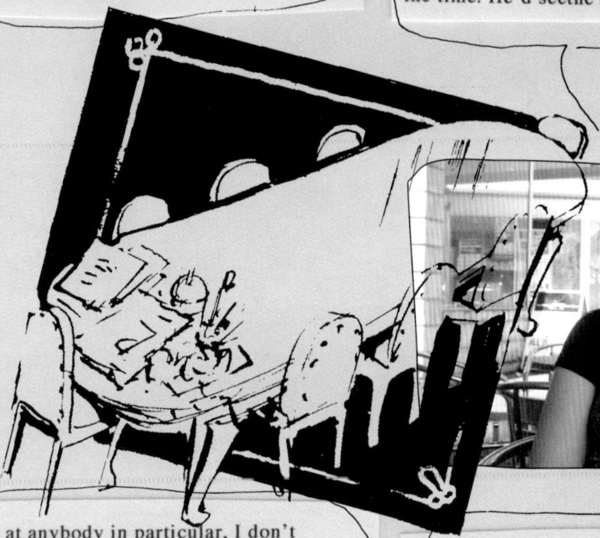

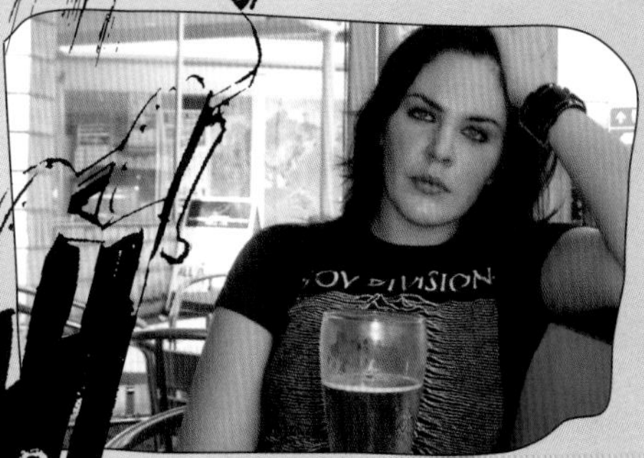

Not at anybody in particular, I don't think. It would just be this colossal accumulating pissoffedness. Dad would be walking out into the street mumbling to himself, cursing some fuckwit who had calmly and innocently written some baloney in Bumfuck, Nowhere.

Kids would be watching him from their windows, waiting for the inevitable moment when he realized he'd forgotten his watch or wallet and he'd curse audibly and go back for it. That could happen up to three or four times in one outing to the supermarket.

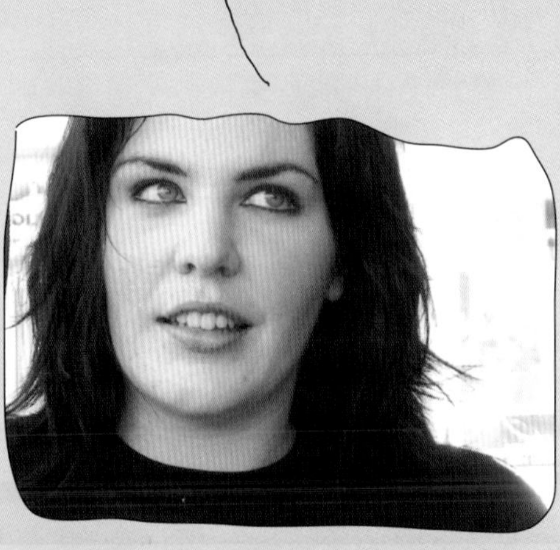

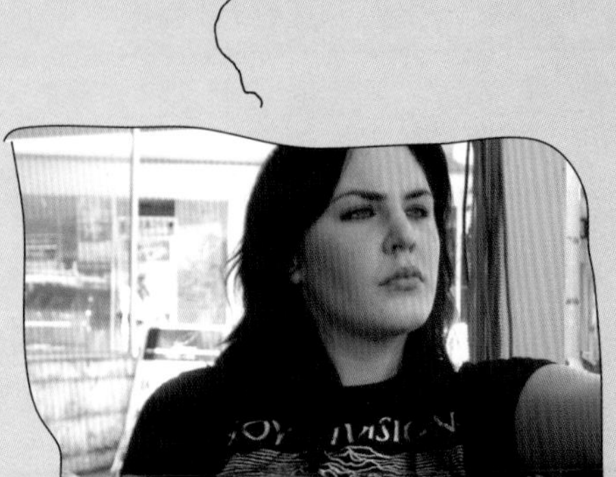

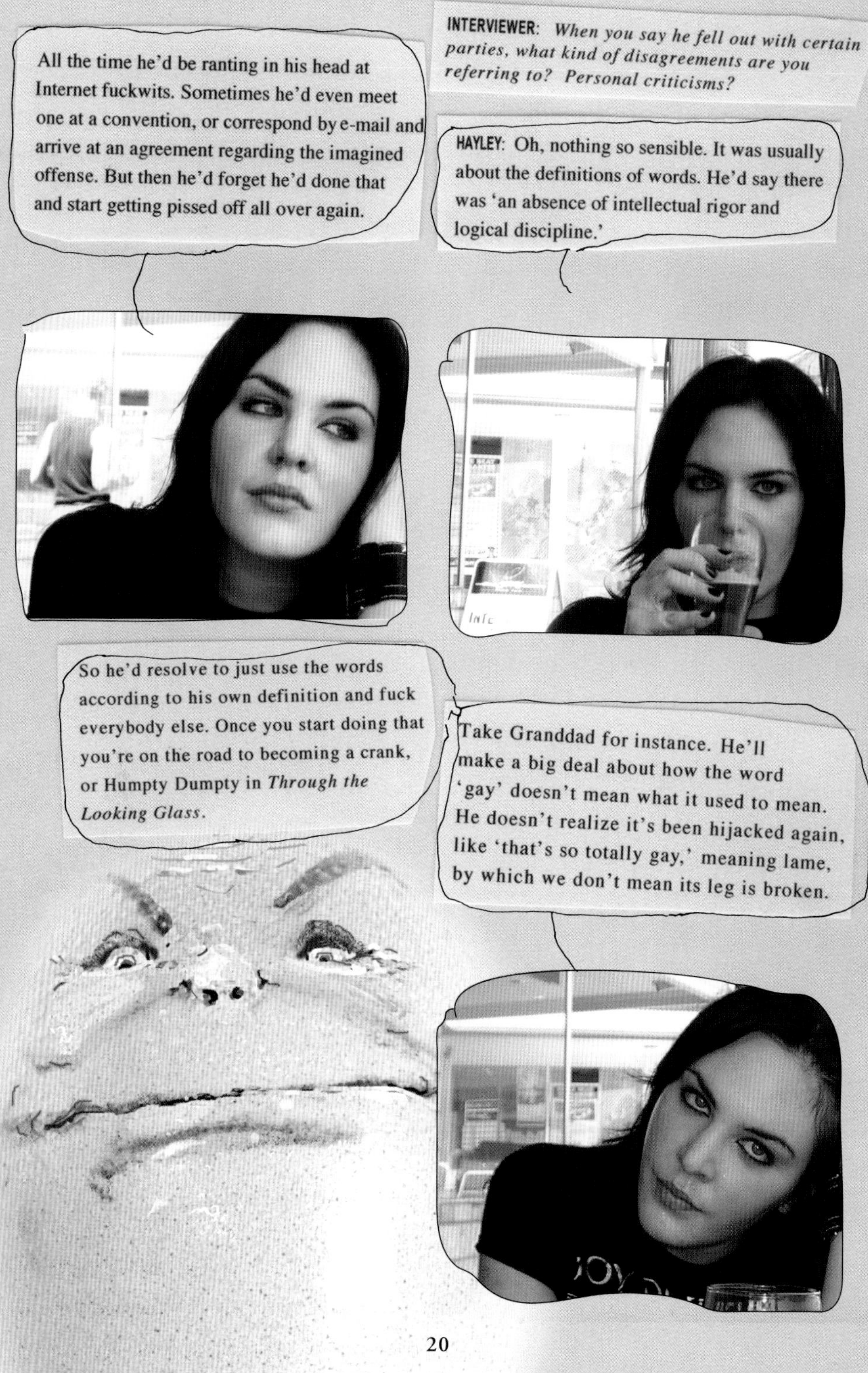
All the time he'd be ranting in his head at Internet fuckwits. Sometimes he'd even meet one at a convention, or correspond by e-mail and arrive at an agreement regarding the imagined offense. But then he'd forget he'd done that and start getting pissed off all over again.
INTERVIEWER: *When you say he fell out with certain parties, what kind of disagreements are you referring to? Personal criticisms?*
HAYLEY: Oh, nothing so sensible. It was usually about the definitions of words. He'd say there was 'an absence of intellectual rigor and logical discipline.'
So he'd resolve to just use the words according to his own definition and fuck everybody else. Once you start doing that you're on the road to becoming a crank, or Humpty Dumpty in *Through the Looking Glass*.
Take Granddad for instance. He'll make a big deal about how the word 'gay' doesn't mean what it used to mean. He doesn't realize it's been hijacked again, like 'that's so totally gay,' meaning lame, by which we don't mean its leg is broken.

So, if he read somebody saying categorically that a comic must have more than one picture or it's not a comic ... You've no idea. That would be a big deal. 'Bloody definers,' he'd say, 'fuck 'em all.' He reserved the right to draw a comic with only one picture if he felt like it. As though somebody was stopping him.

INTERVIEWER: *Could that be the picture he left on the floor of the locker?"*

HAYLEY: There's a thought. Or he'd say he was going to make his 'graphic novel' just a lot of text with a couple of illustrations, as though there was a graphic novel police about to give him a ticket for an imaginary infringement.

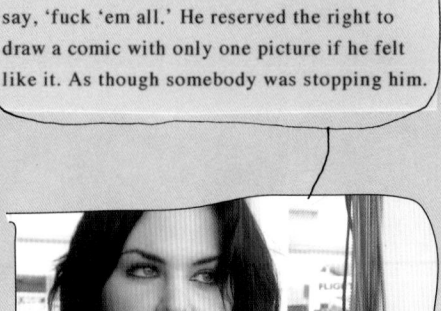

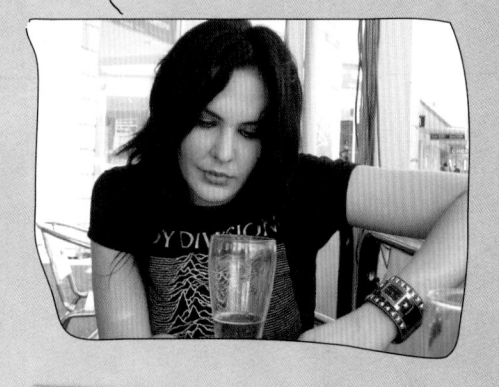

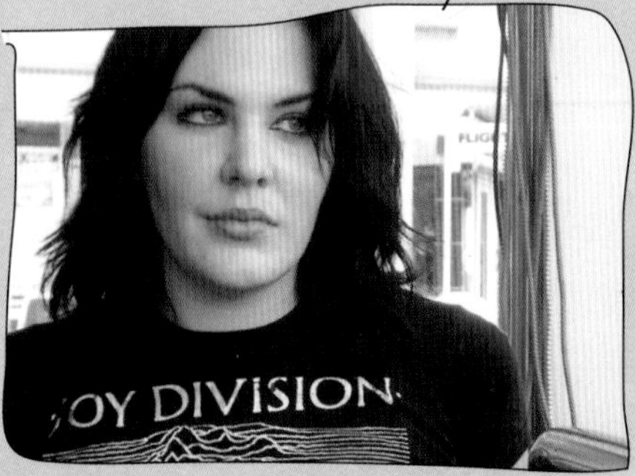

'It's all just illustrated stories,' he'd say, 'And an illustration is just a typographical anomaly.' He detested the way they have to categorize everything. Like Gore Vidal's famous quote "America's obsession with categories has resulted in the creation of two that don't exist: gay and straight."

So he decided in the planet of his head that the words meant one thing and the rest of the universe could go its own confused way. All of this is boring the arse off me having to remember it, because it's hard to believe that anybody gives a shit, but I have to outline it to get to my point.

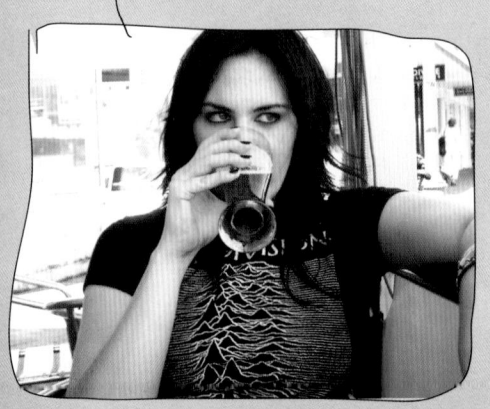

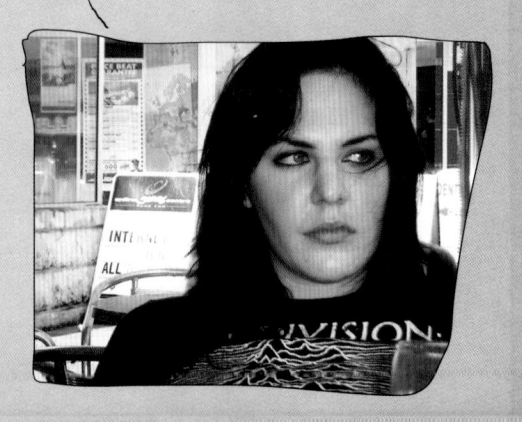

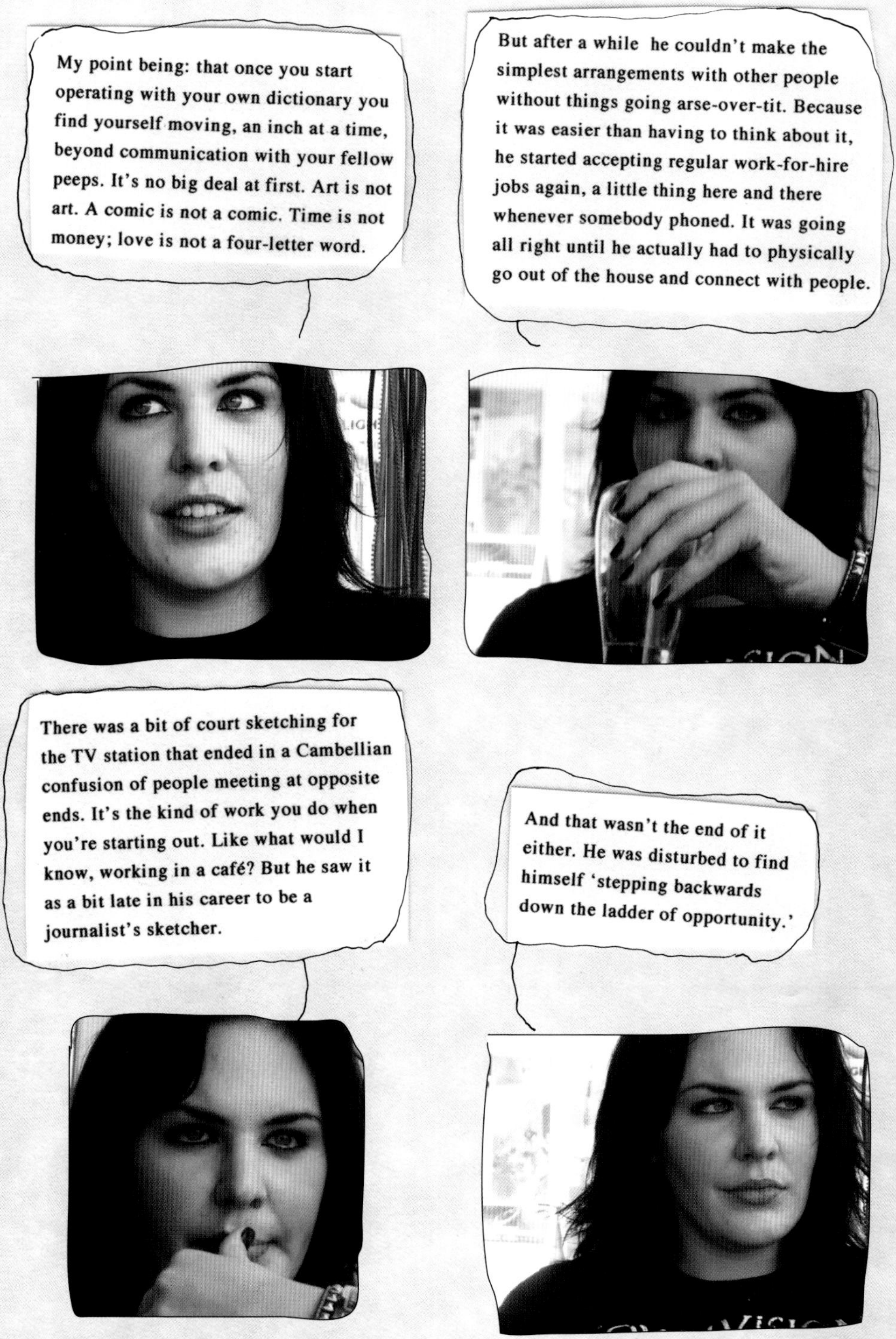
My point being: that once you start operating with your own dictionary you find yourself moving, an inch at a time, beyond communication with your fellow peeps. It's no big deal at first. Art is not art. A comic is not a comic. Time is not money; love is not a four-letter word.
But after a while he couldn't make the simplest arrangements with other people without things going arse-over-tit. Because it was easier than having to think about it, he started accepting regular work-for-hire jobs again, a little thing here and there whenever somebody phoned. It was going all right until he actually had to physically go out of the house and connect with people.
There was a bit of court sketching for the TV station that ended in a Cambellian confusion of people meeting at opposite ends. It's the kind of work you do when you're starting out. Like what would I know, working in a café? But he saw it as a bit late in his career to be a journalist's sketcher.
And that wasn't the end of it either. He was disturbed to find himself 'stepping backwards down the ladder of opportunity.'

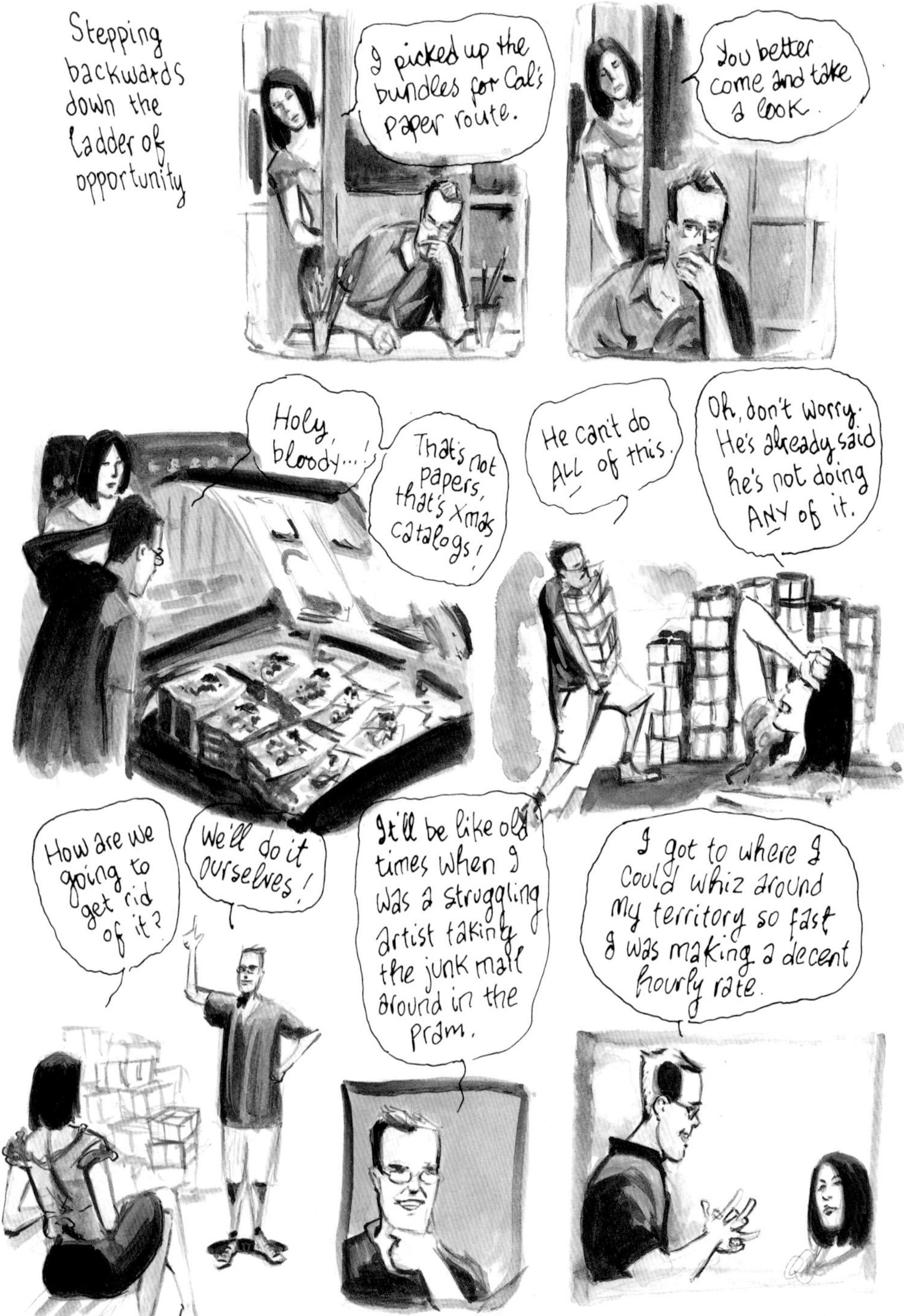
Stepping backwards down the ladder of opportunity
I picked up the bundles for Cal's paper route.
You better come and take a look.
Holy, bloody...!
That's not papers, that's Xmas catalogs!
He can't do ALL of this.
Oh, don't worry. He's already said he's not doing ANY of it.
How are we going to get rid of it?
We'll do it ourselves!
It'll be like old times when I was a struggling artist taking the junk mail around in the pram.
I got to where I could whiz around my territory so fast I was making a decent hourly rate.

The most important thing is the map. What do we have? two territories?

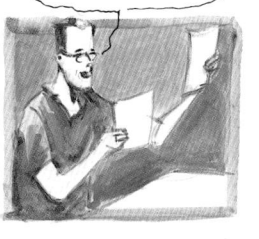

I can divide these maps up so we don't have to double back anywhere

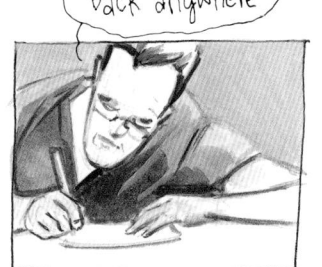

Up this side of the street, down the other.

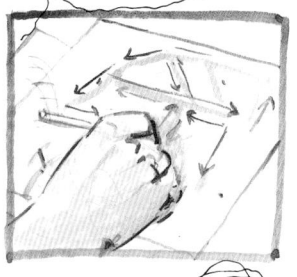

I'll do the carrying. You two do the running

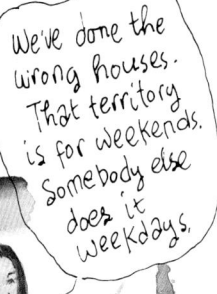

There you have it. Three and a half hours. But why have we run out of books?

I'll find out

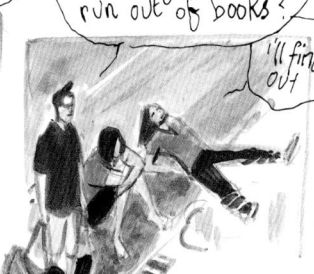

What?

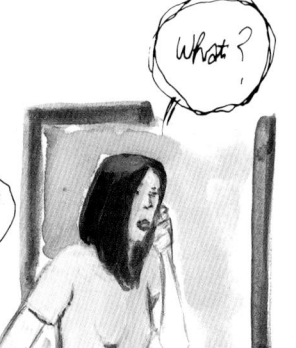

We've done the wrong houses. That territory is for weekends. Somebody else does it weekdays.

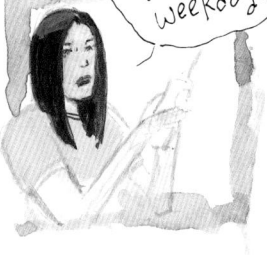

Can we retrieve them? You must be joking!

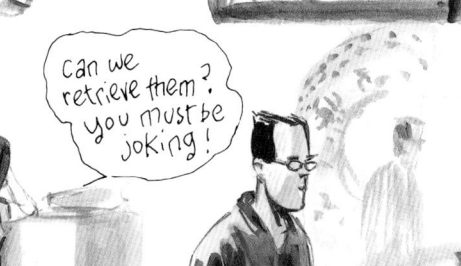

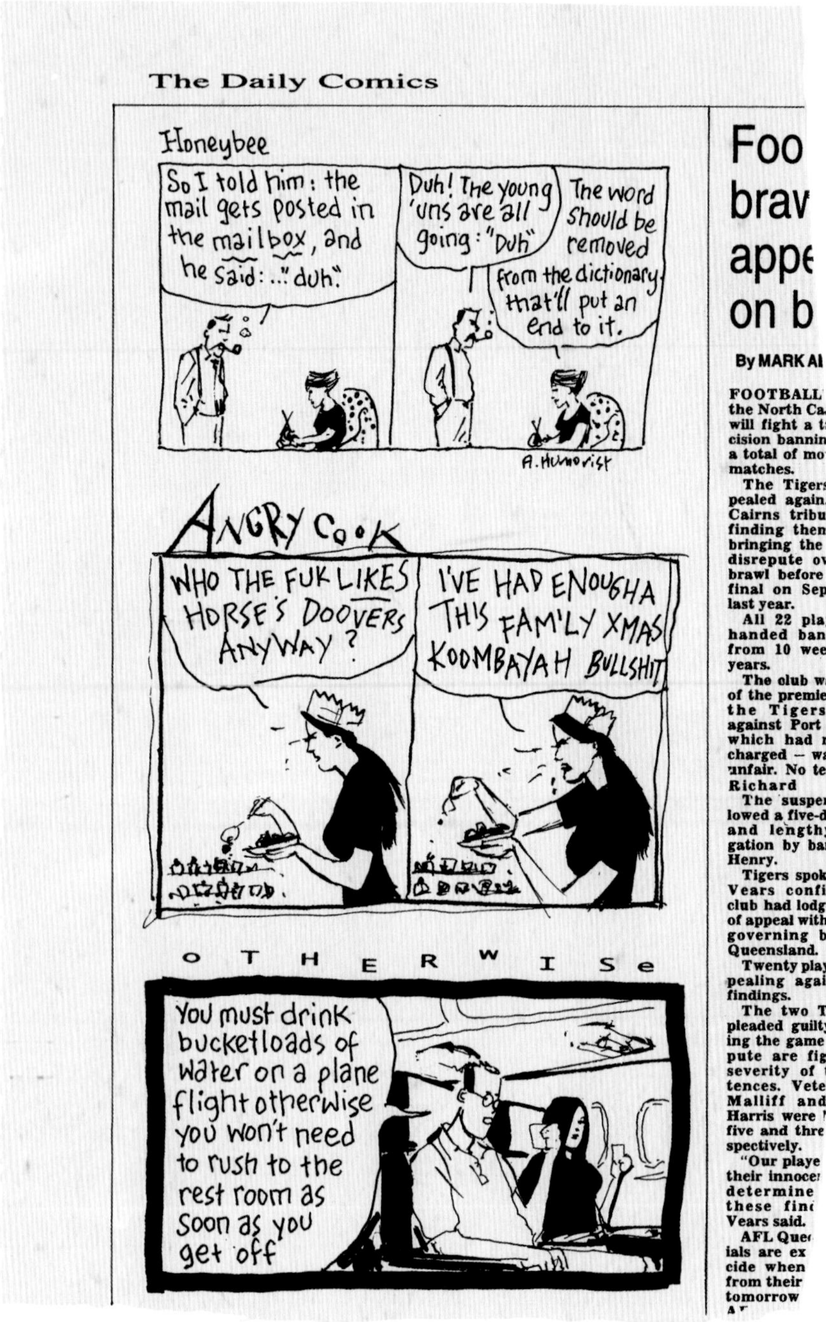
The Daily Comics
Honeybee
So I told him: the mail gets posted in the mailbox, and he said: ..."duh."
Duh! The young 'uns are all going: "Duh"
The word should be removed from the dictionary. that'll put an end to it.
A. Humorist
ANGRY COOK
WHO THE FUK LIKES HORSE'S DOOVERS ANYWAY?
I'VE HAD ENOUGHA THIS FAM'LY XMAS KOOMBAYAH BULLSHIT
OTHERWISE
You must drink bucketloads of water on a plane flight otherwise you won't need to rush to the rest room as soon as you get off
Foo
brav
appe
on b
By MARK AI
FOOTBALL
the North Ca
will fight a t
cision bannin
a total of mo
matches.
The Tigers
pealed again.
Cairns tribu
finding then
bringing the
disrepute ov
brawl before
final on Sept
last year.
All 22 play
handed bans
from 10 week
years.
The club wa
of the premier
the Tigers'
against Port D
which had no
charged – was
unfair. No tean
Richard
The suspensi
lowed a five-day
and lengthy
gation by barr
Henry.
Tigers spokes
Vears confirm
club had lodged
of appeal with t
governing bo
Queensland.
Twenty playe
pealing agai
findings.
The two T
pleaded guilty
ing the game
pute are fig
severity of t
tences. Vete
Malliff and
Harris were
five and thre
spectively.
"Our playe
their innoce
determine
these fin
Vears said.
AFL Que
ials are ex
cide when
from their
tomorrow

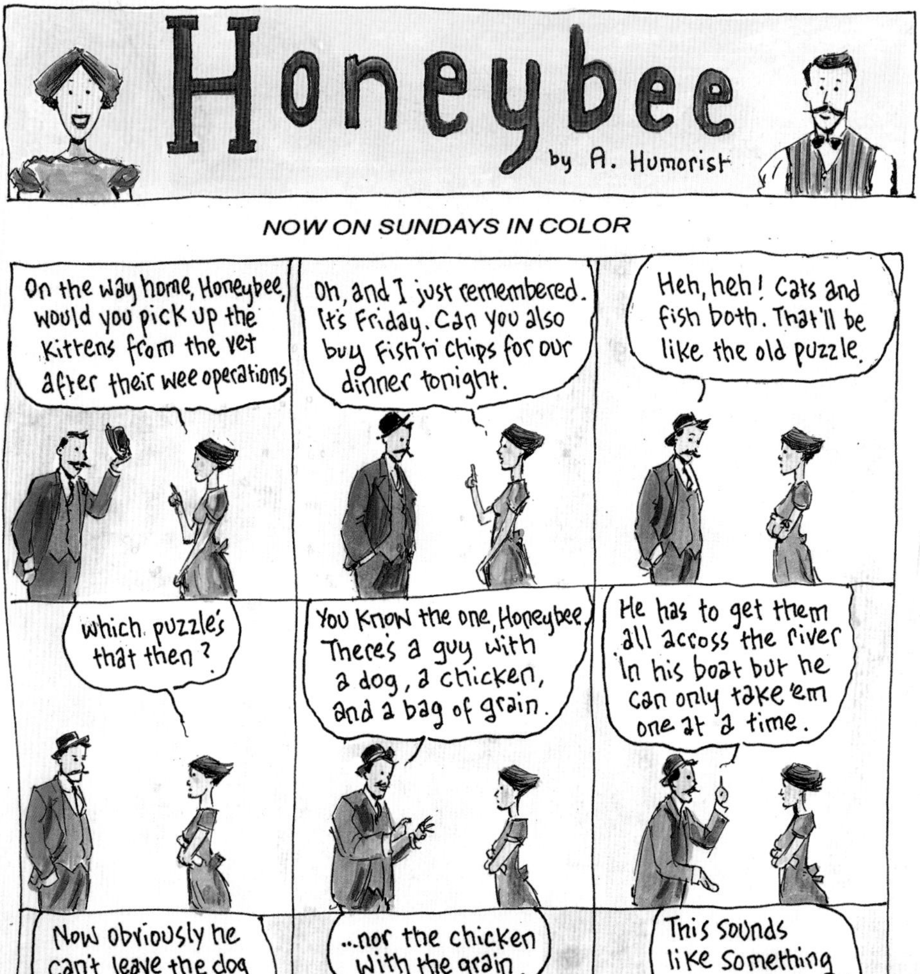
Honeybee
by A. Humorist
NOW ON SUNDAYS IN COLOR
On the way home, Honeybee, would you pick up the Kittens from the vet after their wee operations
Oh, and I just remembered. It's Friday. Can you also buy Fish'n'chips for our dinner tonight.
Heh, heh! Cats and fish both. That'll be like the old puzzle.
which puzzle's that then?
You Know the one, Honeybee. There's a guy with a dog, a chicken, and a bag of grain.
He has to get them all accoss the river in his boat but he can only take 'em one at a time.
Now obviously he can't leave the dog standing with the chicken...
...nor the chicken with the grain.
STOP!
This sounds like something YOU organized!

Page 4

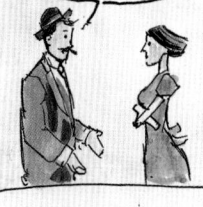

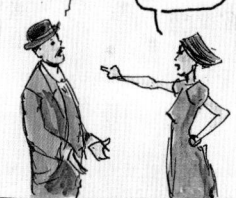

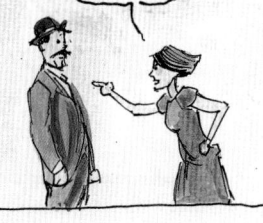

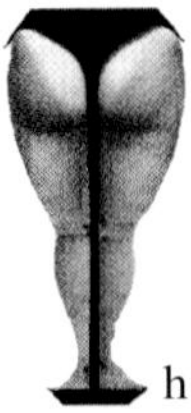

The accountant's waiting room is an art gallery. His office is an art gallery too. The accountant is the major exhibit.

He's wearing a sarong decorated with frangipani. I shake his hand.

Mothertucker Management makes a specialty of dealing with creative people: actors, writers, artists ... the lot.

Brian Tucker doesn't look like an accountant. But then, some say I don't look like a detective.

I eye the works hanging around the white interior. I cast my line: "Do any of your clients ever pay you in ordinary cash?"

He looks around, quizzical. "Oh, the pictures. I do occasionally buy a piece from a client."

"Did Campbell ever try to pay you with a picture?"

"Well, if he did I wouldn't say. At least until the police make an official investigation. Though if he's missing for good I should definitely have bought a piece from him at the right time."

"What do you mean by that?"

"Uh, that was a joke, in reference to the popular misconception that an artist's value goes through the roof after he dies."

"Is that so? I never–"

"Hmm ... stuff of comedy. You probably don't know the old movie in which Dick Van Dyke played a struggling artist in Paris who staged his own death in order to raise the prices of his work."

"Hey, maybe I'll rent the video."

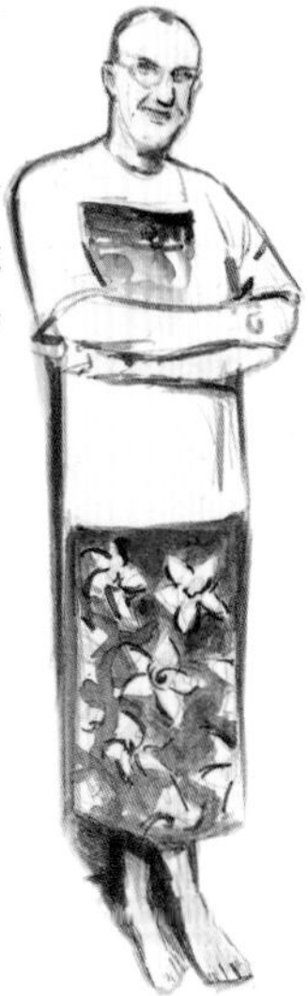

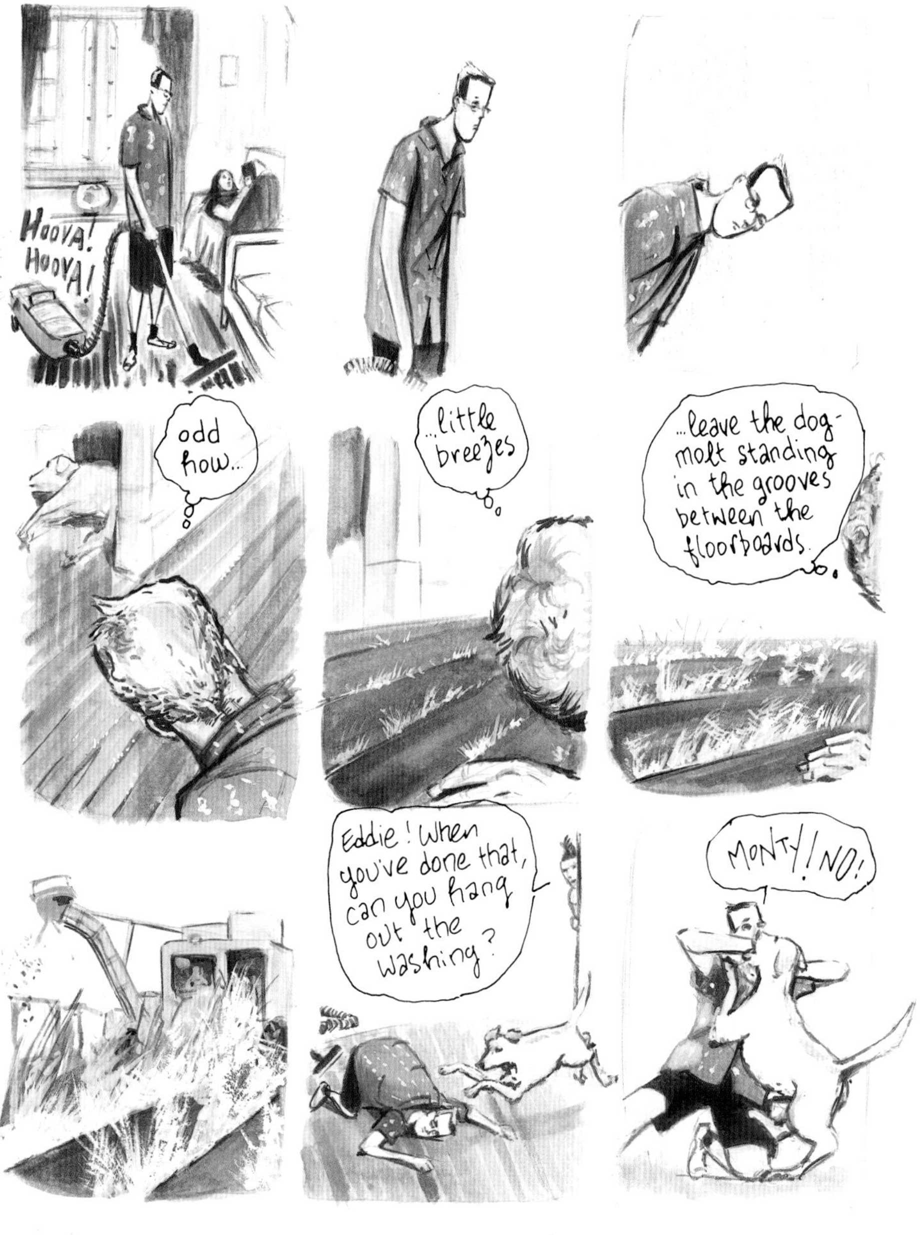
HOOVA! HOOVA!
odd how...
...little breezes
...leave the dog-molt standing in the grooves between the floorboards.
Eddie! When you've done that, can you hang out the washing?
MONTY! NO!

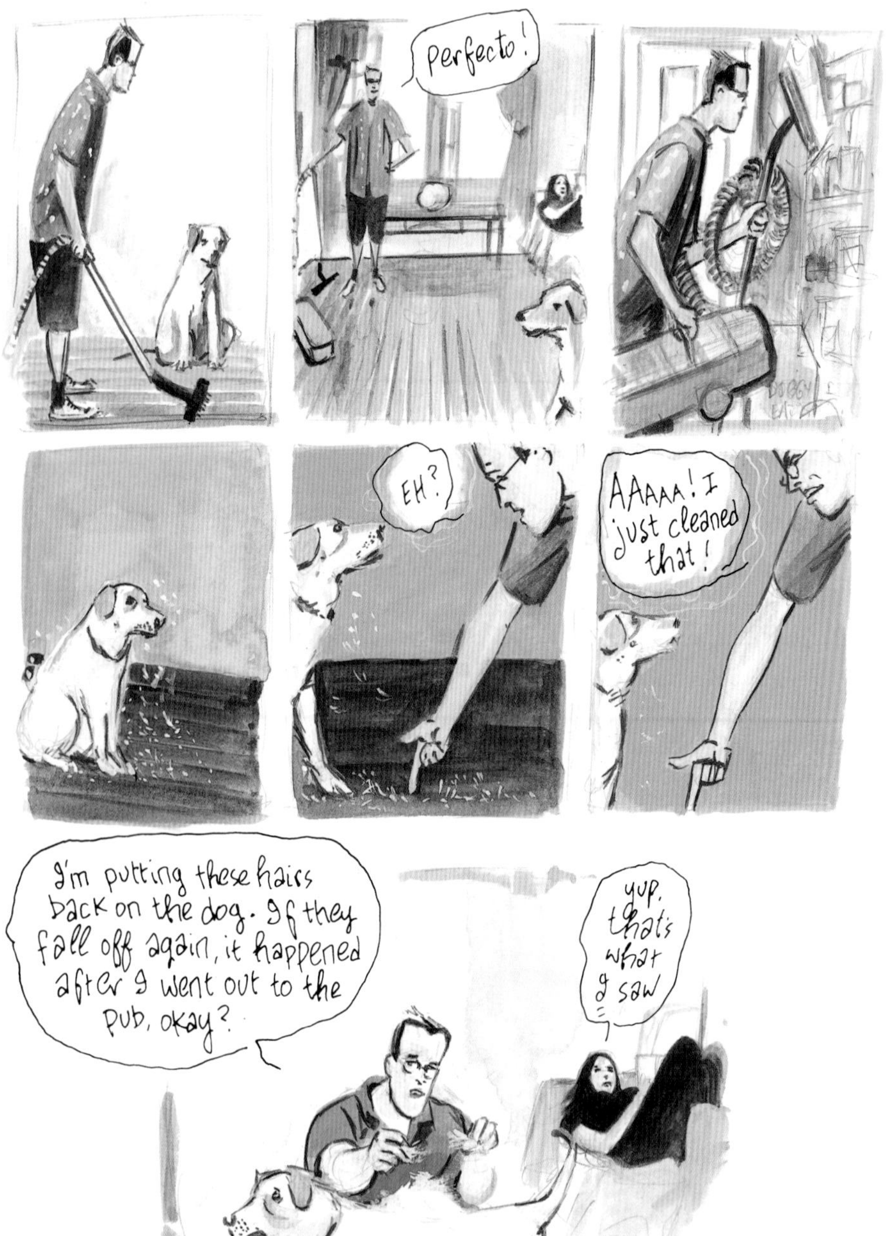
Perfecto!
EH?
AAAAA! I just cleaned that!
I'm putting these hairs back on the dog. If they fall off again, it happened after I went out to the pub, okay?
yup, that's what I saw

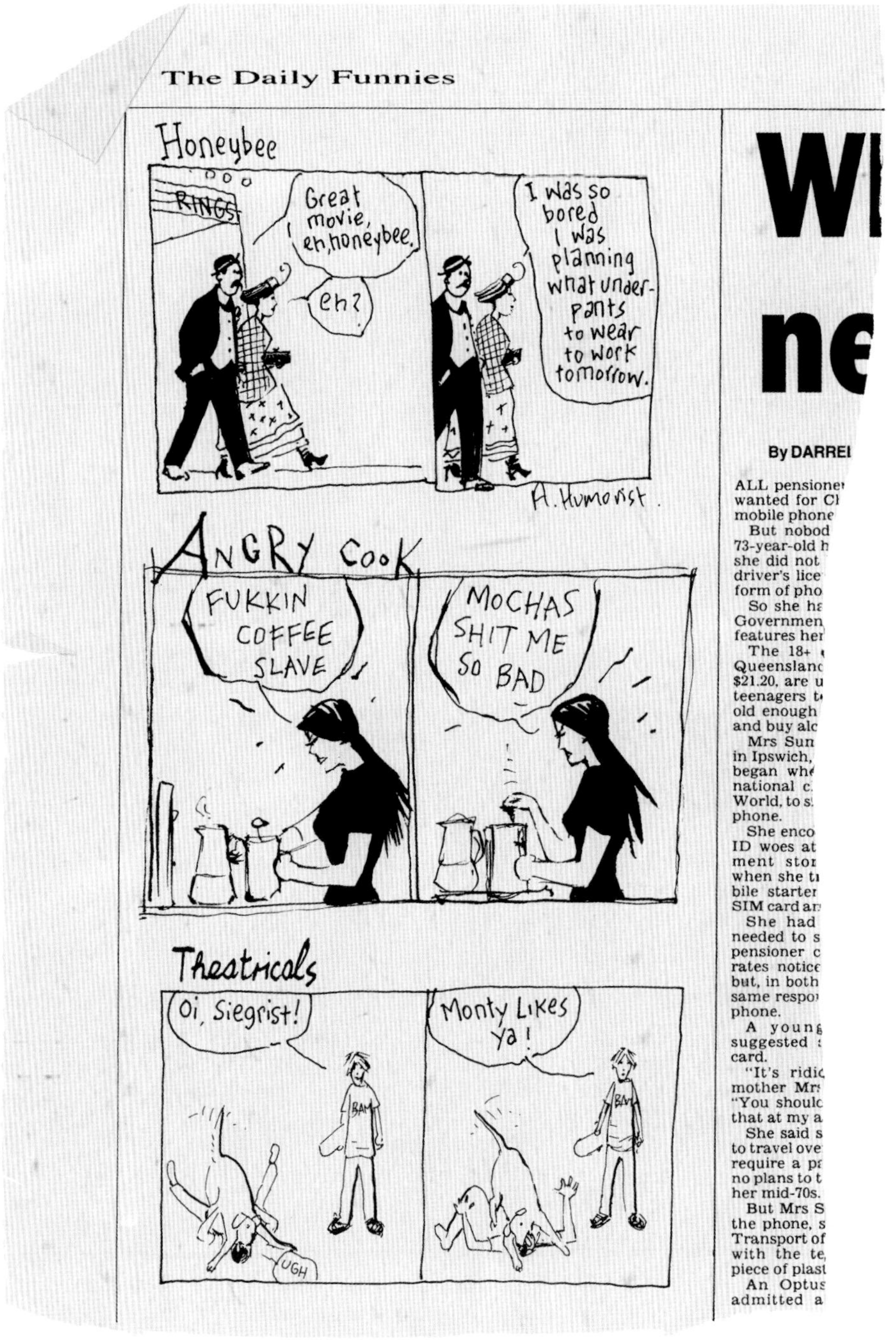
The Daily Funnies
Honeybee
RINGS
Great movie, eh,honeybee.
eh?
I was so bored I was planning what under-pants to wear to work tomorrow.
A. Humorist.
ANGRY COOK
FUKKIN COFFEE SLAVE
MOCHAS SHIT ME SO BAD
Theatricals
Oi, Siegrist!
UGH
Monty Likes ya!
BAM
BAM
Wl
ne
By DARREI
ALL pensione
wanted for Cl
mobile phone
But nobod
73-year-old h
she did not
driver's lice
form of pho
So she ha
Governmen
features her
The 18+
Queenslanc
$21.20, are u
teenagers t
old enough
and buy alc
Mrs Sun
in Ipswich,
began whe
national c
World, to s
phone.
She enco
ID woes at
ment stor
when she t
bile starter
SIM card ar
She had
needed to s
pensioner c
rates notice
but, in both
same respo
phone.
A young
suggested
card.
"It's ridic
mother Mr
"You shoulc
that at my a
She said s
to travel ove
require a p
no plans to t
her mid-70s.
But Mrs S
the phone, s
Transport of
with the te
piece of plast
An Optus
admitted a

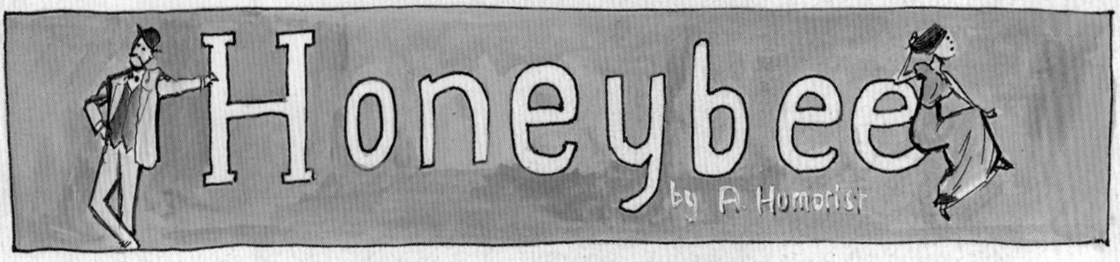
Honeybee
by A. Humorist

IN OUR COLOR SUPPLEMENT EVERY SUNDAY

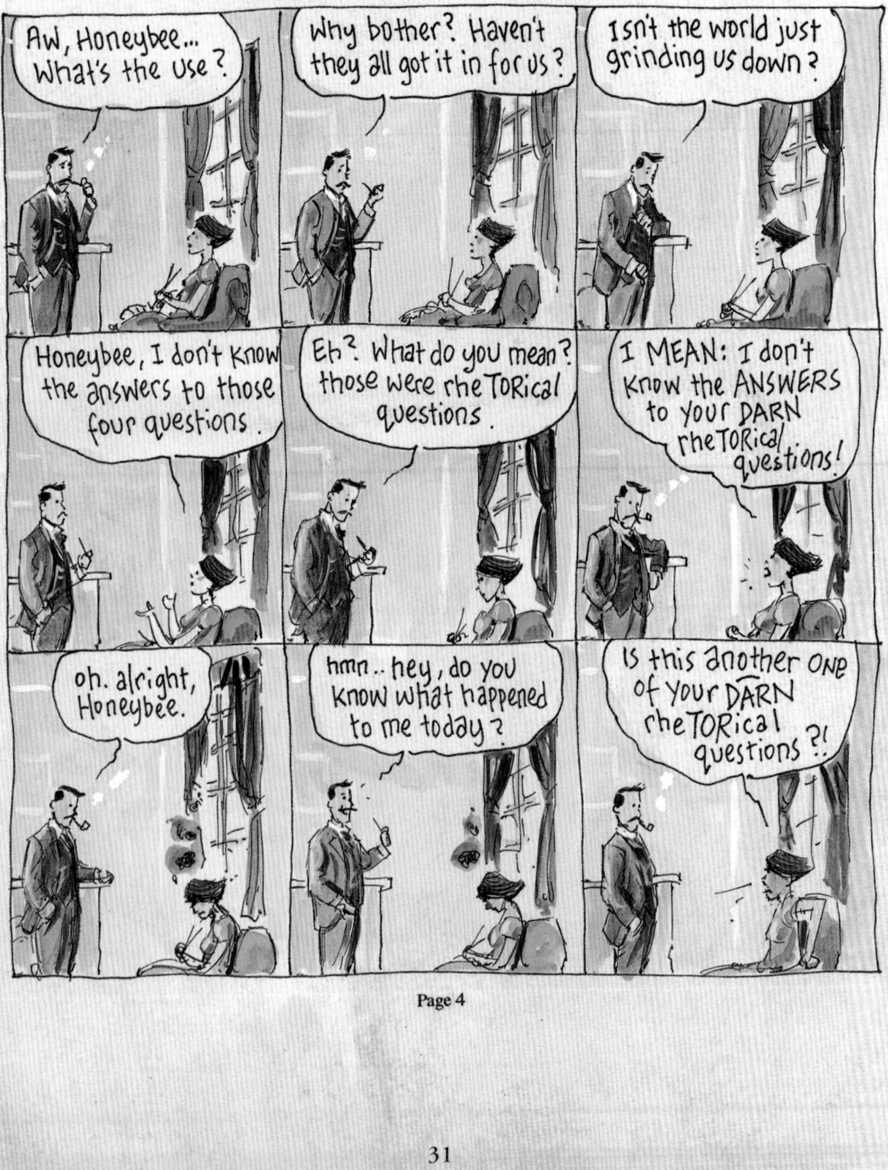
Aw, Honeybee... What's the use?
Why bother? Haven't they all got it in for us?
Isn't the world just grinding us down?
Honeybee, I don't know the answers to those four questions.
Eh? What do you mean? those were rheTORical questions.
I MEAN: I don't know the ANSWERS to your DARN rheTORical questions!
oh. alright, Honeybee.
hmn.. hey, do you know what happened to me today?
Is this another one of your DARN rheTORical questions?!

Page 4

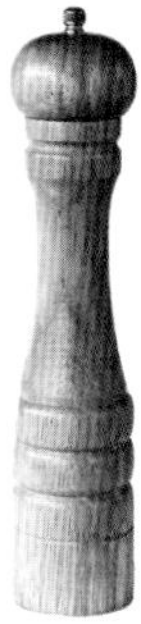

lug the big black plastic bags up to the house and go through enough of them to get the picture."It's just arch-lever files. Maybe seventy or more, all packed full of loose leaves in those transparent packets with the holes at the side; correspondence, clippings." I'm not telling them anything they don't already know. "He was really precious about this stuff, wasn't he?"

"Well that's his archives, bagged to 'keep out the beasties,'" answers the daughter, putting on a Scots accent whenever the opportunity presents itself.

"Though the funny thing is, we once found a dead 'beastie' that looked like a holy manifestation. 'Our Lady of the squashed cockroach' we called it. I took it to school for my art project. Mrs. Walpole wasn't impressed."

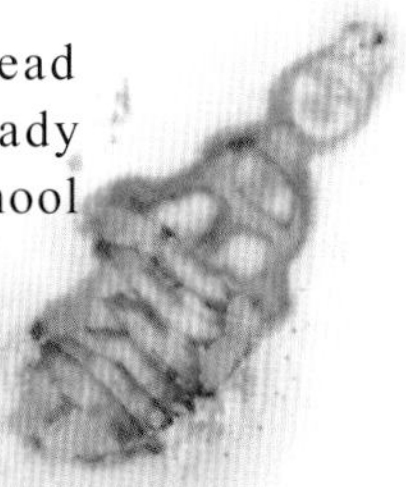

"But they were more than just clippings to him." It's the wife's turn again. "He was ordering the universe. Or that's what he thought. Sometimes he'd cut pages out of one book and transfer them to another. We've got a three-volume illustrated medical encyclopedia. You'll be looking up the common cold and suddenly there will be a hole in the page because there was an eighteenth-century skit on cowpox on the reverse. Or some perfectly useful information on diet during pregnancy will have been sacrificed to the priority of filing a reproduction of a French phrenological lithograph where it will make more sense only to Campbell.

"He'd cut them to fit, because he was a neatness fanatic, but you'd think a true neatness nut would want the pages in the book they came in.

"Then he might decide that some pages made more sense in another file and he'd start shifting them. Sometimes he'd take the entire contents of one file and swap them with the entire contents of a different file. It made no sense. The black bags used to be in the bedroom. Occasionally I'd hear a rustling in the middle of the night and I'd know that paper was on the move."

"Sometimes," says the daughter, "Fate would back him up by fixing it so that a random photo could cause a huge kerfuffle. Like that night Marlene came to stay."

"But didn't."

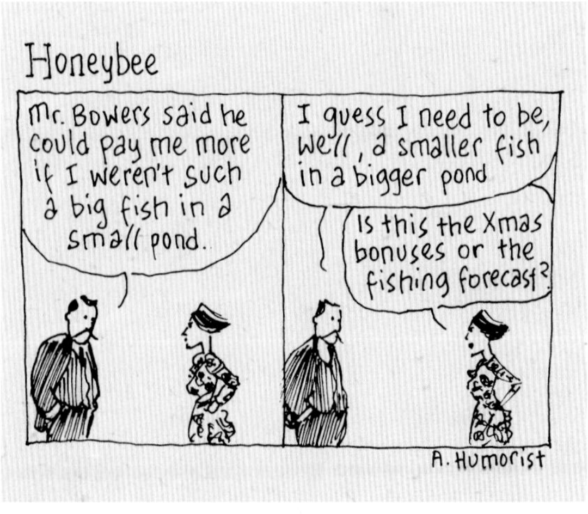
Honeybee
Mr. Bowers said he could pay me more if I weren't such a big fish in a small pond.
I guess I need to be, well, a smaller fish in a bigger pond
Is this the Xmas bonuses or the fishing forecast?
A. Humorist

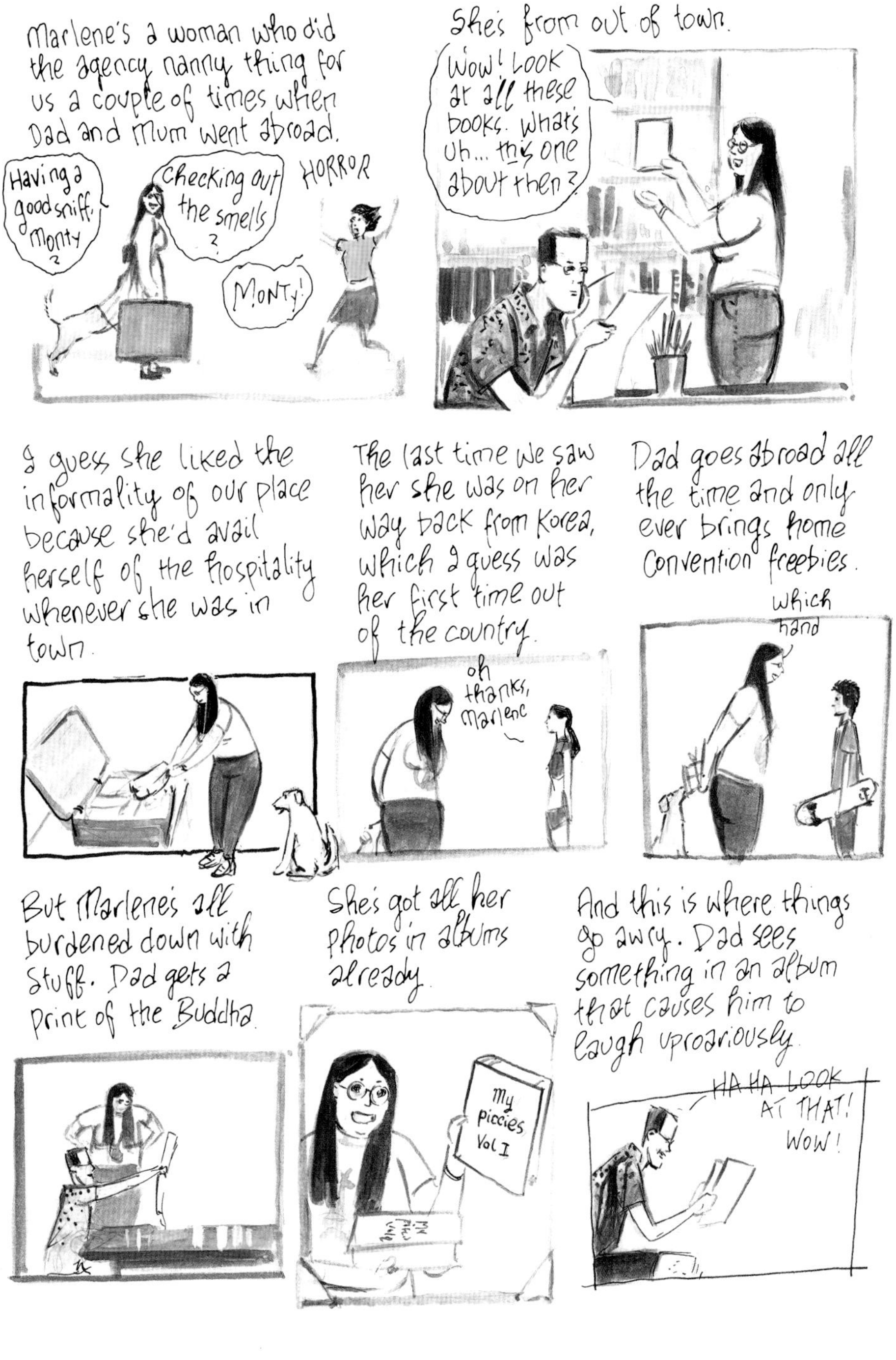
Marlene's a woman who did the agency nanny thing for us a couple of times when Dad and Mum went abroad.
Having a good sniff, Monty?
Checking out the smells?
HORROR
MONTY!
She's from out of town.
Wow! LOOK at all these books. What's uh... this one about then?
I guess she liked the informality of our place because she'd avail herself of the hospitality whenever she was in town.
The last time we saw her she was on her way back from Korea, which I guess was her first time out of the country.
oh thanks, Marlene
Dad goes abroad all the time and only ever brings home convention freebies.
which hand
But Marlene's all burdened down with stuff. Dad gets a print of the Buddha
She's got all her photos in albums already.
My piccies Vol I
And this is where things go awry. Dad sees something in an album that causes him to laugh uproariously.
HA HA LOOK AT THAT! WOW!

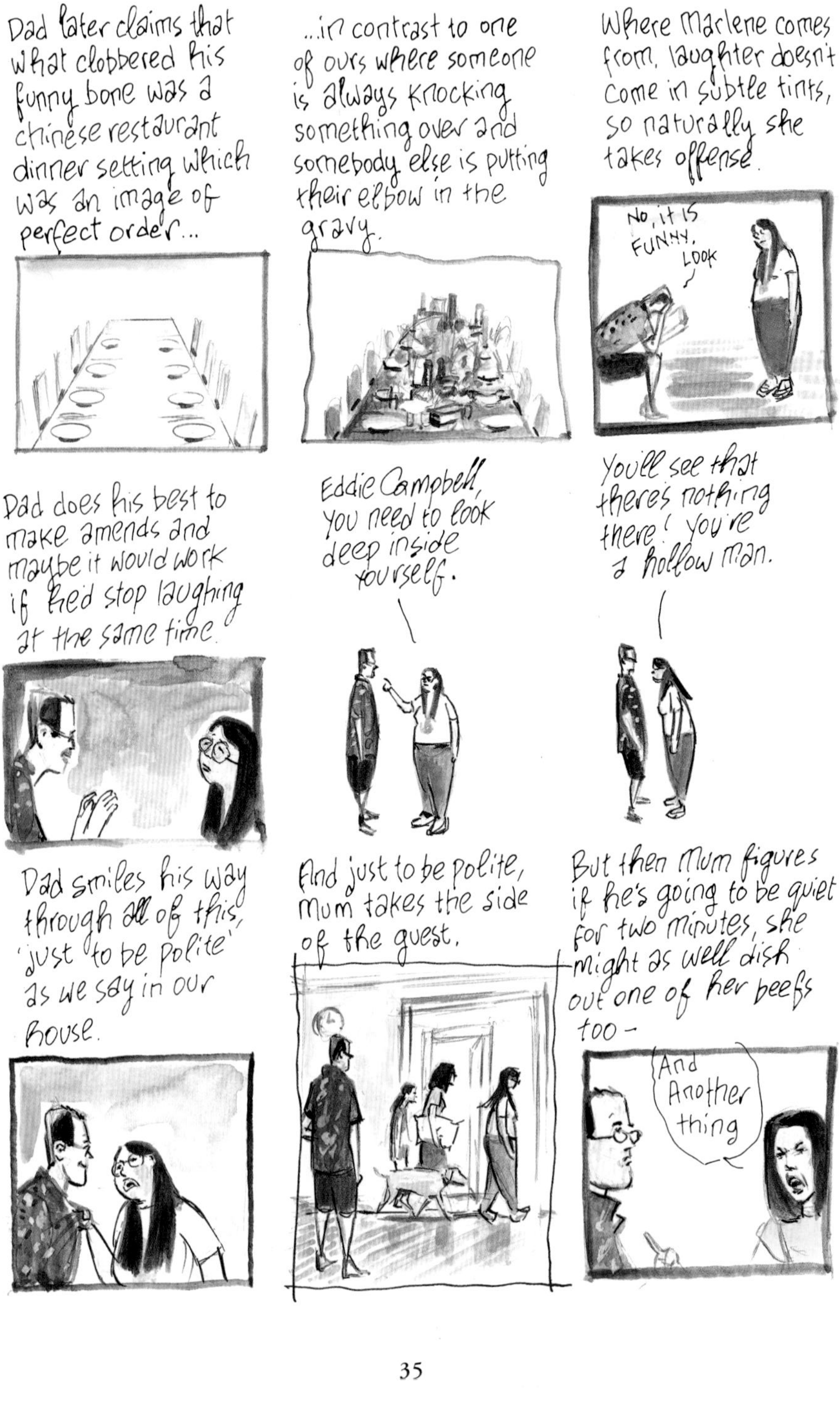
Dad later claims that what clobbered his funny bone was a chinese restaurant dinner setting which was an image of perfect order...
...in contrast to one of ours where someone is always knocking something over and somebody else is putting their elbow in the gravy.
Where Marlene comes from, laughter doesn't come in subtle tints, so naturally she takes offense.
No, it is funny.
Look
Dad does his best to make amends and maybe it would work if he'd stop laughing at the same time.
Eddie Campbell, you need to look deep inside yourself.
You'll see that there's nothing there! You're a hollow man.
Dad smiles his way through all of this, 'just to be polite' as we say in our house.
And just to be polite, Mum takes the side of the guest.
But then Mum figures if he's going to be quiet for two minutes, she might as well dish out one of her beefs too –
And Another thing

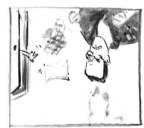

Now that he's been made into the cornered beast, you can't really expect him to keep up the politeness.

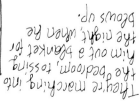

They're marching into the bedroom, tossing him out a blanket for the night, when he blows up.

YOU! OUT!

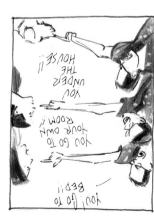

You go to bed!!

YOU GO TO YOUR OWN ROOM!!

YOU UNDER THE HOUSE!!

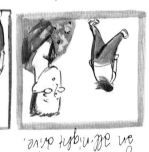

Marlene decides to go home, which is an all-night drive.

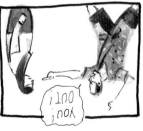

Dad's belatedly trying to contain the situation by hiding her suitcase.

I'm calling the police!

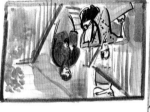

she gets her way and departs. Dad helps her out with her case.

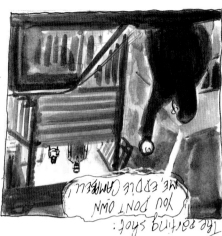

The parting shot:

YOU DON'T OWN ME, EDDIE CAMPBELL

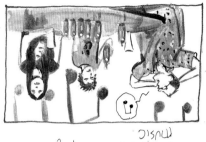

One day it'll get a psychologist to explain it all to me. Meanwhile, Dad gives us all a beer and plays loud music.

At the same time as he thought art should reveal the order in the universe, he couldn't understand the idea of ordering your garden, so Mum usually got a man in to mow the lawn. People are daft about lawns where we are. They usually know the names of all the species of grasses and aim for a uniform surface, but Dad's lawn was made up of at least five different grasses including but not limited to: broadleaf, blue couch, fescue, rye, and pubic.

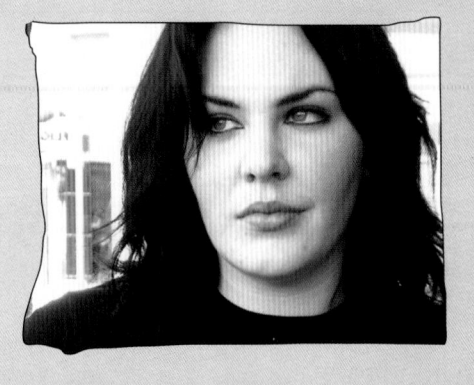

MISSED A BIT
?
MONUMENT TO CHAOS
DO NOT MOW WITHIN A FOOT

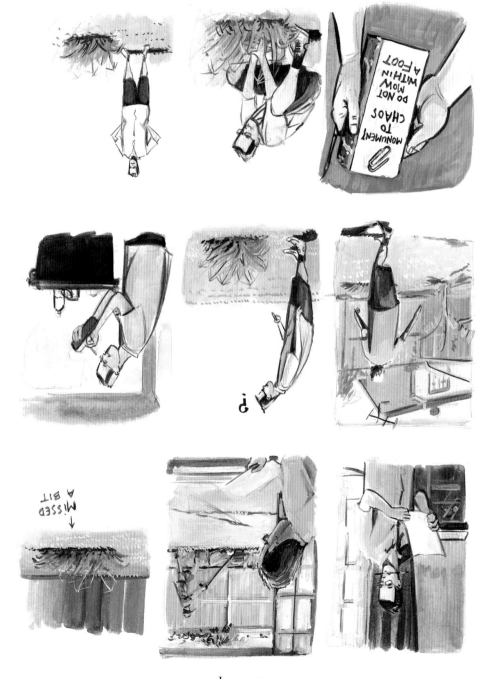

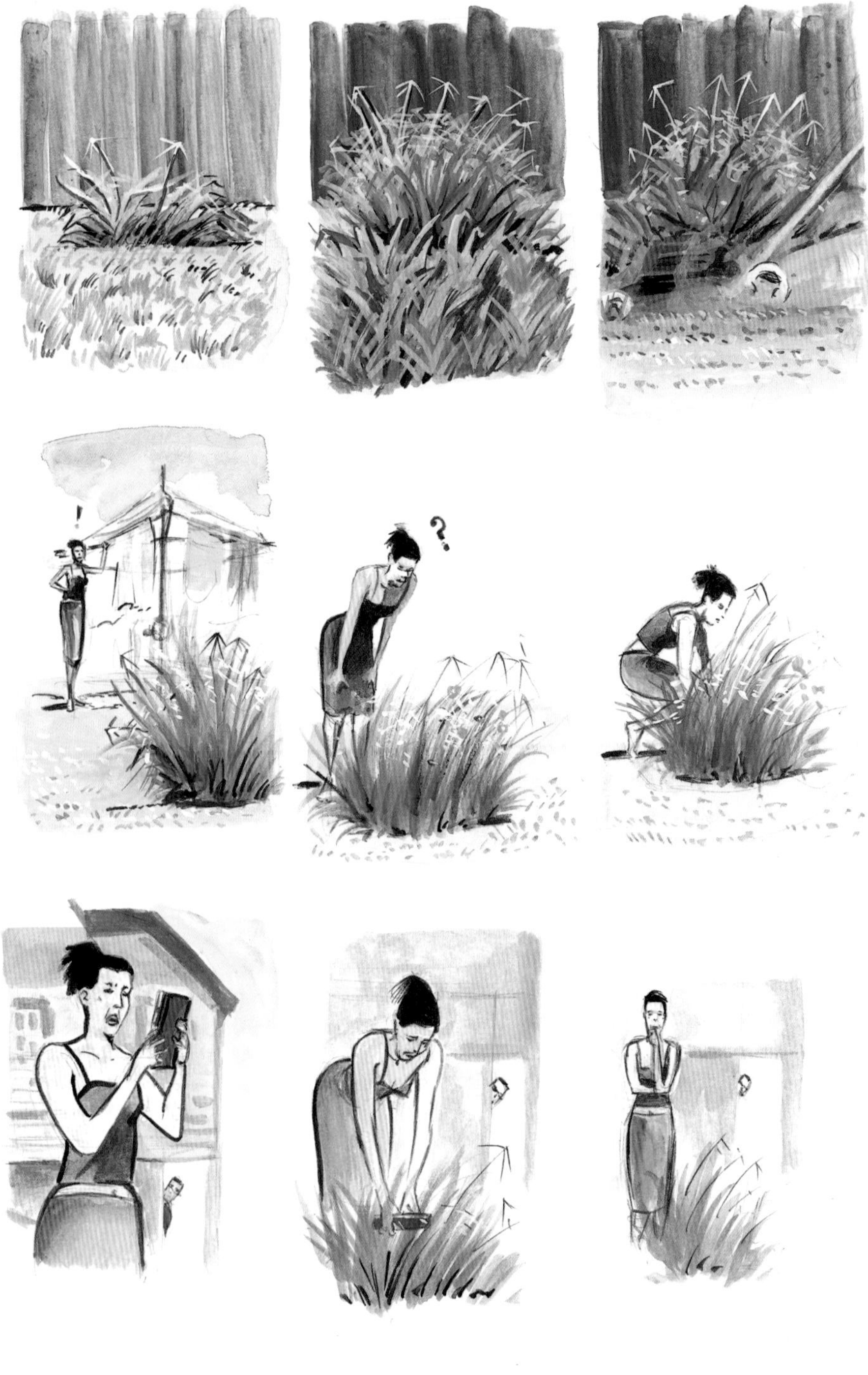
!
?

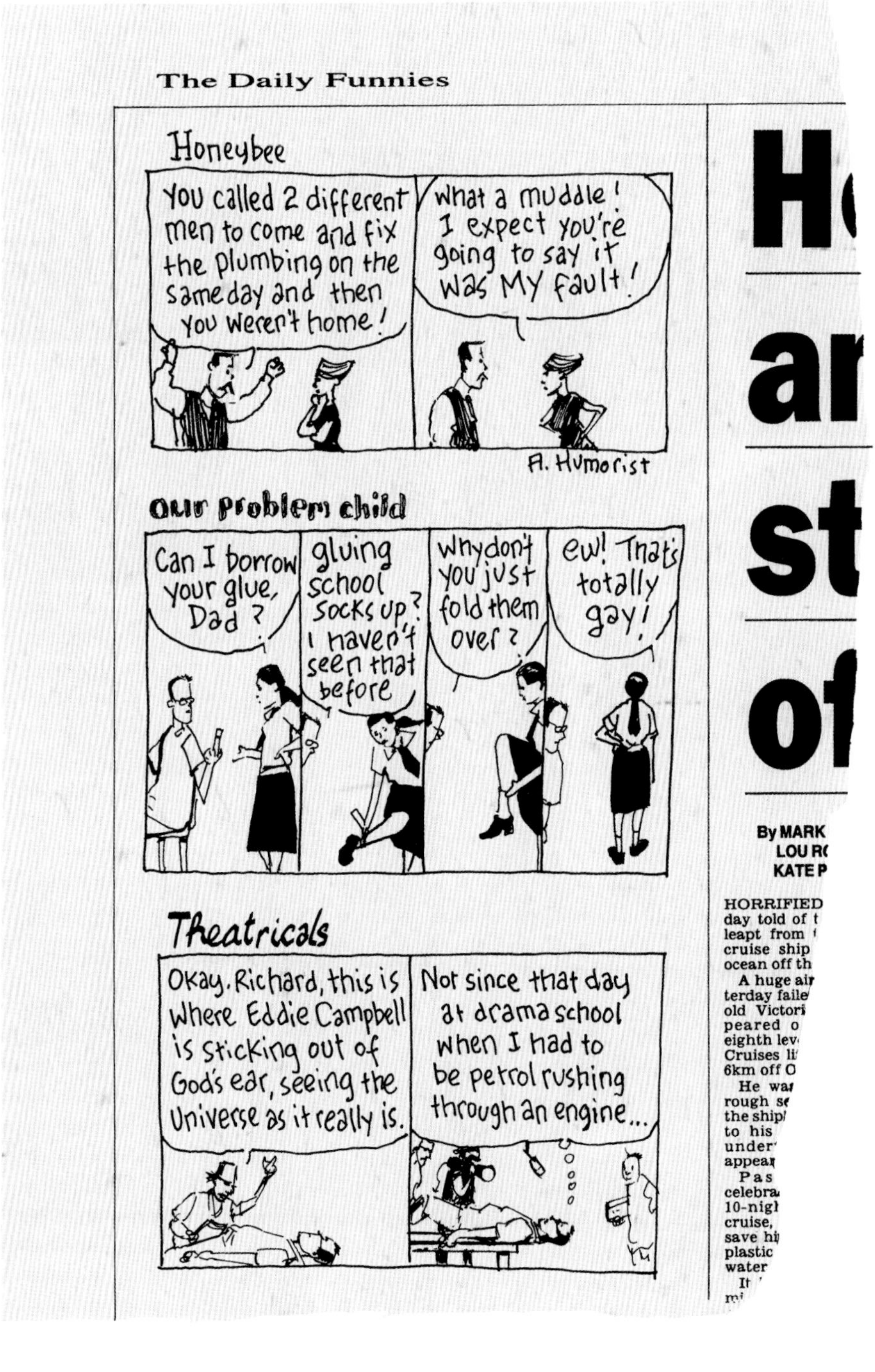
The Daily Funnies
Honeybee
You called 2 different men to come and fix the plumbing on the same day and then you weren't home!
What a muddle! I expect you're going to say it was my fault!
A. Humorist
Our problem child
Can I borrow your glue, Dad?
gluing school socks up? I haven't seen that before
why don't you just fold them over?
ew! That's totally gay!
Theatricals
Okay. Richard, this is where Eddie Campbell is sticking out of God's ear, seeing the Universe as it really is.
Not since that day at drama school when I had to be petrol rushing through an engine...
By MARK
LOU R
KATE P
HORRIFIED
day told of
leapt from
cruise ship
ocean off th
A huge ai
terday faile
old Victori
peared o
eighth lev
Cruises li
6km off O
He wa
rough s
the ship
to his
under
appea
Pas
celebr
10-nig
cruise,
save hi
plastic
water

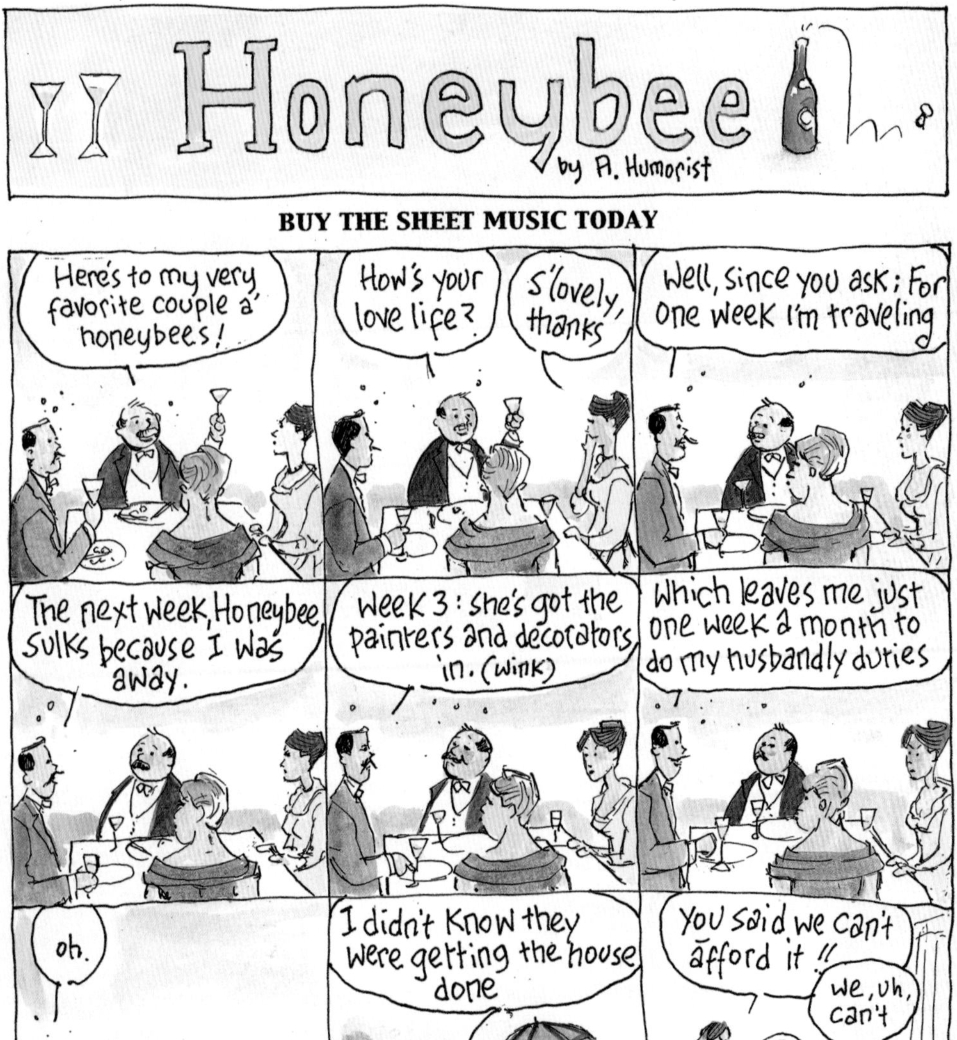
Honeybee
by A. Humorist
BUY THE SHEET MUSIC TODAY
Here's to my very favorite couple a' honeybees!
How's your love life?
S'lovely, thanks
Well, since you ask; For one week I'm traveling
The next week, Honeybee sulks because I was away.
Week 3: she's got the painters and decorators in. (wink)
Which leaves me just one week a month to do my husbandly duties
oh.
I didn't know they were getting the house done
You said we can't afford it!!
we, uh, can't

Page 4

eave us well provided for? Well, he left us with a lot of windows that don't close properly and a fridge towel," complains the wife, leaving it to the daughter to explain why fridges need towels.

"The fridge has been leaking water onto the floor for months. Years, probably. Nobody can remember when it started. But instead of getting it fixed we now have a permanent 'fridge towel' to mop up the water. It gets washed and then put back in place on the kitchen floor. It drives Mum mad. She was always threatening to get a 'man' in, and she always said it like that, with the quotation marks."

"Then there's the 'door spoon.' When the handle came off the pantry door, before anyone had time to screw it back on, it got lost. So now we have a spoon hanging on a nail on the wall, for prying the door open. Then there's the 'TV poker,' the 'tap screamer,' the 'phone sock'... "

"He was so arrogantly superior to all the ordinary stuff."

"Hmm, I don't know about that. Sometimes he seemed to be sneaking around all the time thinking he was getting away with something, hoping to escape the notice of the intergalactic headmaster. I mean, did he never learn to drive because in order to get a license, he'd have to bow to somebody else's authority, or was it because in some part of his head he's not convinced he's the right age yet?"

"Remember he used to have a light for his bicycle? Pete gave it to him years ago, but the battery ran out and he never got around to replacing it. So now, when he's out at night he sneaks along the footpaths in the dark like a big possum."

"Another one of his daft ideas was that you shouldn't trust anyone who has all the right gear for the job. I think he meant those wallies who can't just ride a bike but have to wear the skin-tight Lycra and the water bottle, and the aerodynamic helmet."

"Yeh, he only ever had that polystyrene one, all bashed up and perched on the back of his noggin. It would have been useless in a crash. Mum always said it looked like an 'esky.' And his head was so big we could carry all the salad and drinks in it and call it the 'picnic helmet."

"Except you could never get him out into the country for that sort of thing. If he's done a runner, that's the last place you'll find him."

"That's right. One of his art assistants once invited him and Mum to be their guests at a mountain retreat. Now anybody else would have been h a p p y to get a weekend 'out bush,' but not Dad. Of course he nodded in all the right places. He even gave away tickets to a concert he'd bought for the Saturday night ...

"What I meant was, did he have life insurance?"

"He always said–"

"Mum! He's eliminating you from his inquiries."

"What do you mean?"

"He's checking you didn't bump Dad off."

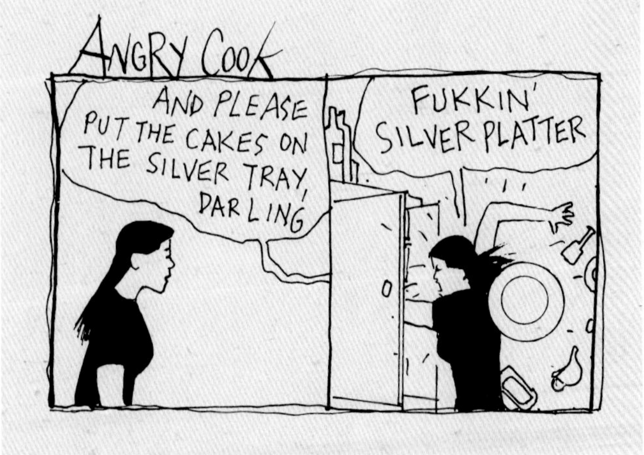
ANGRY COOK
AND PLEASE PUT THE CAKES ON THE SILVER TRAY, DARLING
FUKKIN' SILVER PLATTER

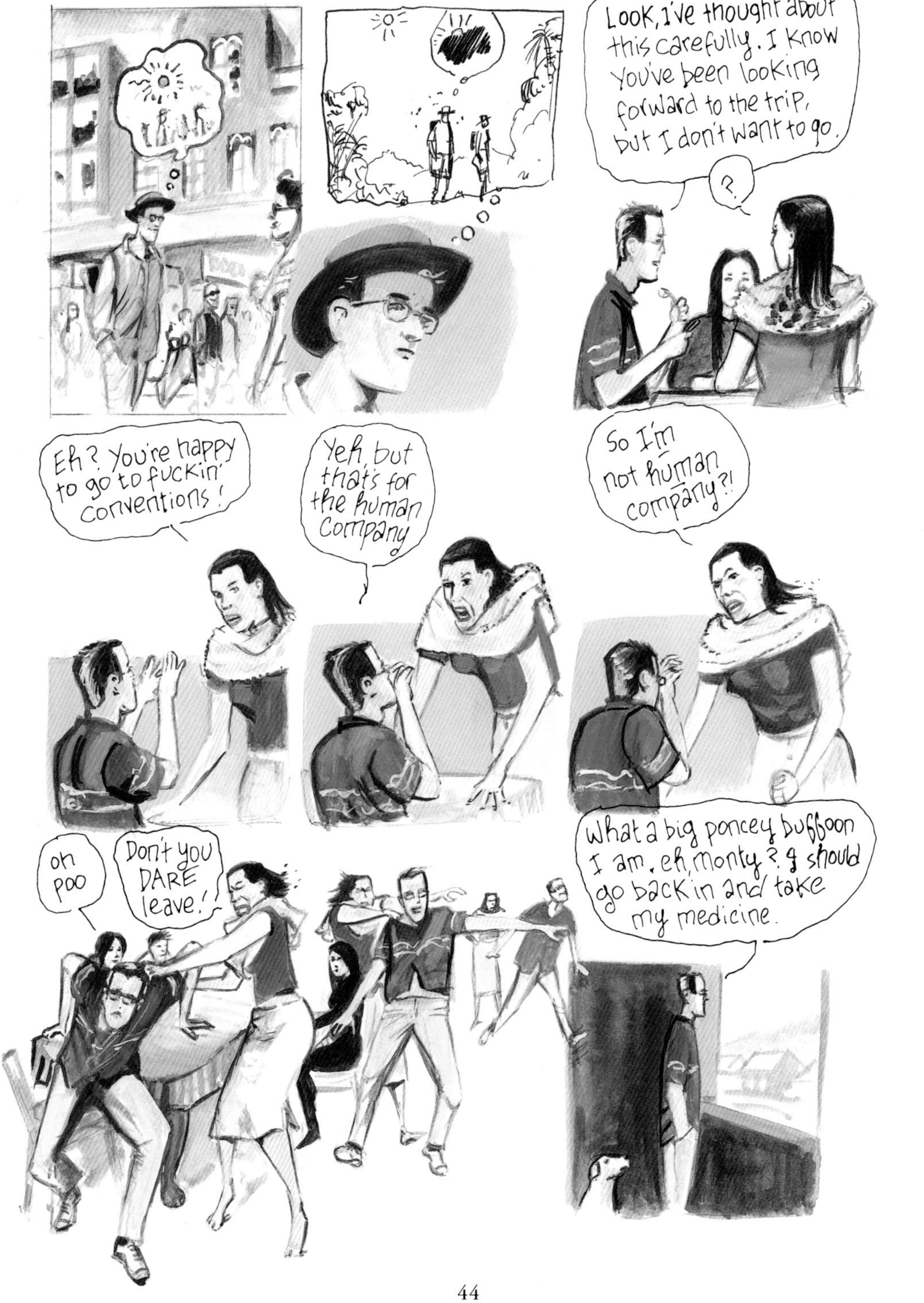
Look, I've thought about this carefully. I know you've been looking forward to the trip, but I don't want to go.
?
Eh? You're happy to go to fuckin' conventions!
Yeh, but that's for the human company
So I'm not human company?!
oh poo
Don't you DARE leave!
What a big poncey buffoon I am, eh, Monty? I should go back in and take my medicine.

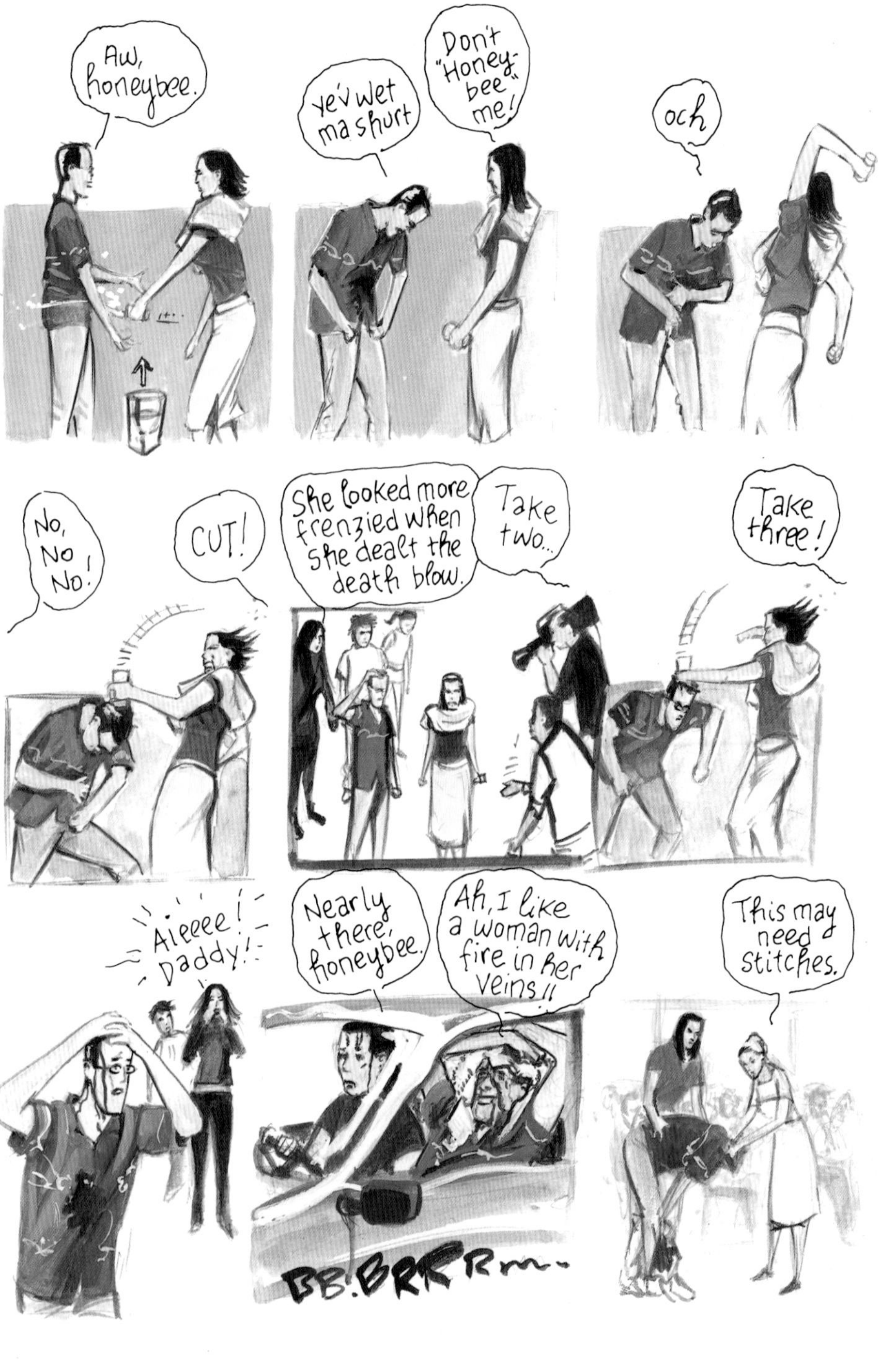
Aw, honeybee.
ye'v wet ma shurt
Don't "Honey-bee" me!
och
No, No No!
CUT!
She looked more frenzied when she dealt the death blow.
Take two...
Take three!
Aieeee! Daddy!
Nearly there, honeybee.
Ah, I like a woman with fire in her veins!!
BB.BRKRm..
This may need stitches.

INTERLUDE

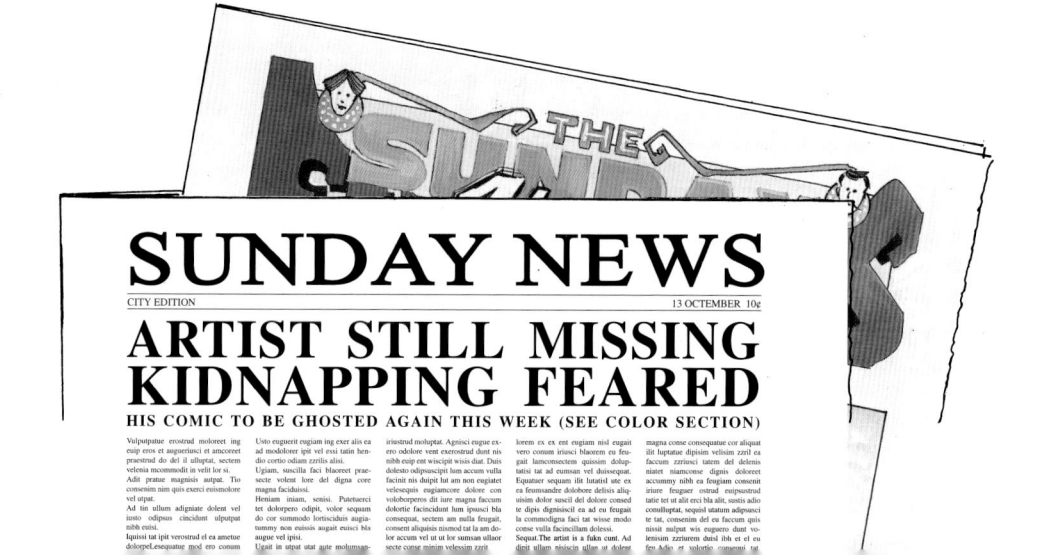

SUNDAY NEWS

CITY EDITION   13 OCTEMBER 10g

ARTIST STILL MISSING
KIDNAPPING FEARED

HIS COMIC TO BE GHOSTED AGAIN THIS WEEK (SEE COLOR SECTION)

Vulpiriputpatue erostrud moloreet ing euip eros et augueriaci et amceeret praestrud do del il ulluptat, sectem velenia mcommodit in velit lor si. Adit pratue magnisis autpat. Tuo consenim nim quis exerci euismolore vel utpat.

Ad tin ullum adigniate dolent vel iusto odipsus cincidunt ulputpat nibh euisi.

Iquissi tat ipit verostrud el ea ametue dolorpeLesequatue mol ero conum

Usto euguerit eugiam ing exer alis ea ad modeloret ipit vel essi tatin hendio cortio odiam zzrilis alisi.

Ugiam, suscilla faci blaoreet praesecte volent fore del digna core magna faciduisi.

Heniam iniam, senisi. Patetuerci tet dolorpero odipit, volor sequam do cor summodo fortisciduis augiatummy non euissis augait euisci bis augue vel ipisi.

Ugait in utpat utat aute molumsan-

iriustrud moluptat. Agnisci eugue exero odolore vent exerostrud dunt nis nibh euip ent wiscipit wisis diat. Duis dolesto odipsuscipit lum accum vulla facinit nis duipit lut am non eugiatet velesequis eugiamcore dolore con voloborperos dit iure magna faccum dofortie facincidunt lum ipsusci bla consequat, sectem am nulla feugait, consent aliquisis nismod tat la am dolor accum vel ut ut lor sumsan ullaor secte cunse minim velessim zzrit

lorem ex ex ent eugiam nisl eugait vero conum iriusci blaorem eu feugait lamcotsectem quissim doluptatisi tat ad eumsan vel duissequat. Equatuer sequam ilit lutatisl ent ex ea feumsandre dolobore delisis aliquisim dolor suscil del dolore consed te dipis dignissicil ea ad eu feugait in commodigna faci tat wisse modo conse vulla facincillam dolessi.

Sequat.The artist is a fukn cunt. Ad dipit ullum nisiscin ullan ut dolent

magna conse consequate cor aliquat ilit luptatue dipisim velisim zzril ea faccum zzriusci tatem del delenis niatet niamcome dignis doloreet accumny nibh ea feugiam consenit iriure feuguer estrud euipsustrud tatie tet ut alit erci bla alit, ustis adio conulluptat, sequisl statum adipsusci te tat, consenim del ea faccum quis nissit nulput wis euguero dunt volensuim zzrtarem dutsl ibh et el eu fen Adio et volortio consenist tat

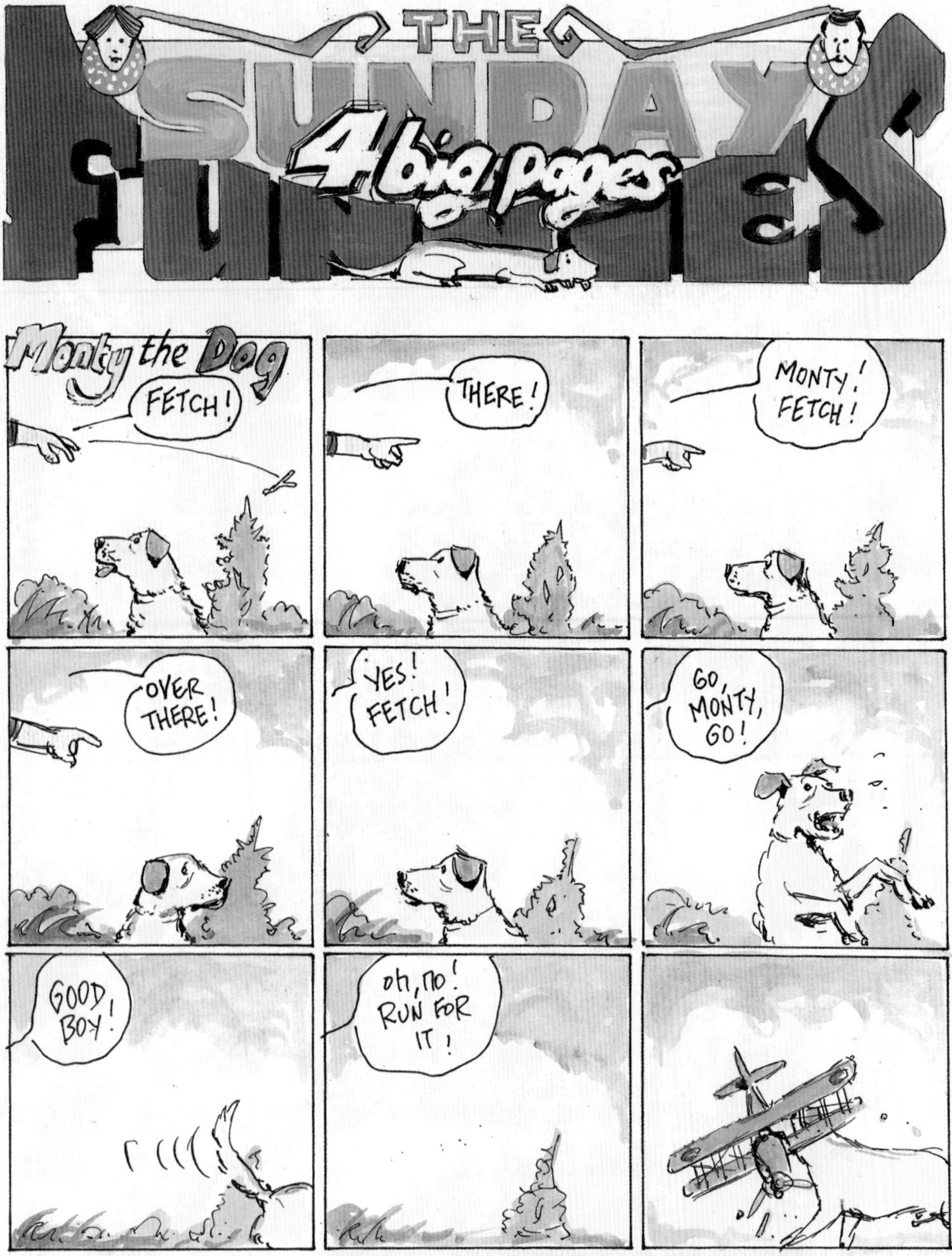
THE
SUNDAY
FUNNIES
4 big pages
Monty the Dog
FETCH!
THERE!
MONTY! FETCH!
OVER THERE!
YES! FETCH!
GO, MONTY, GO!
GOOD BOY!
OH, NO! RUN FOR IT!

Page 1

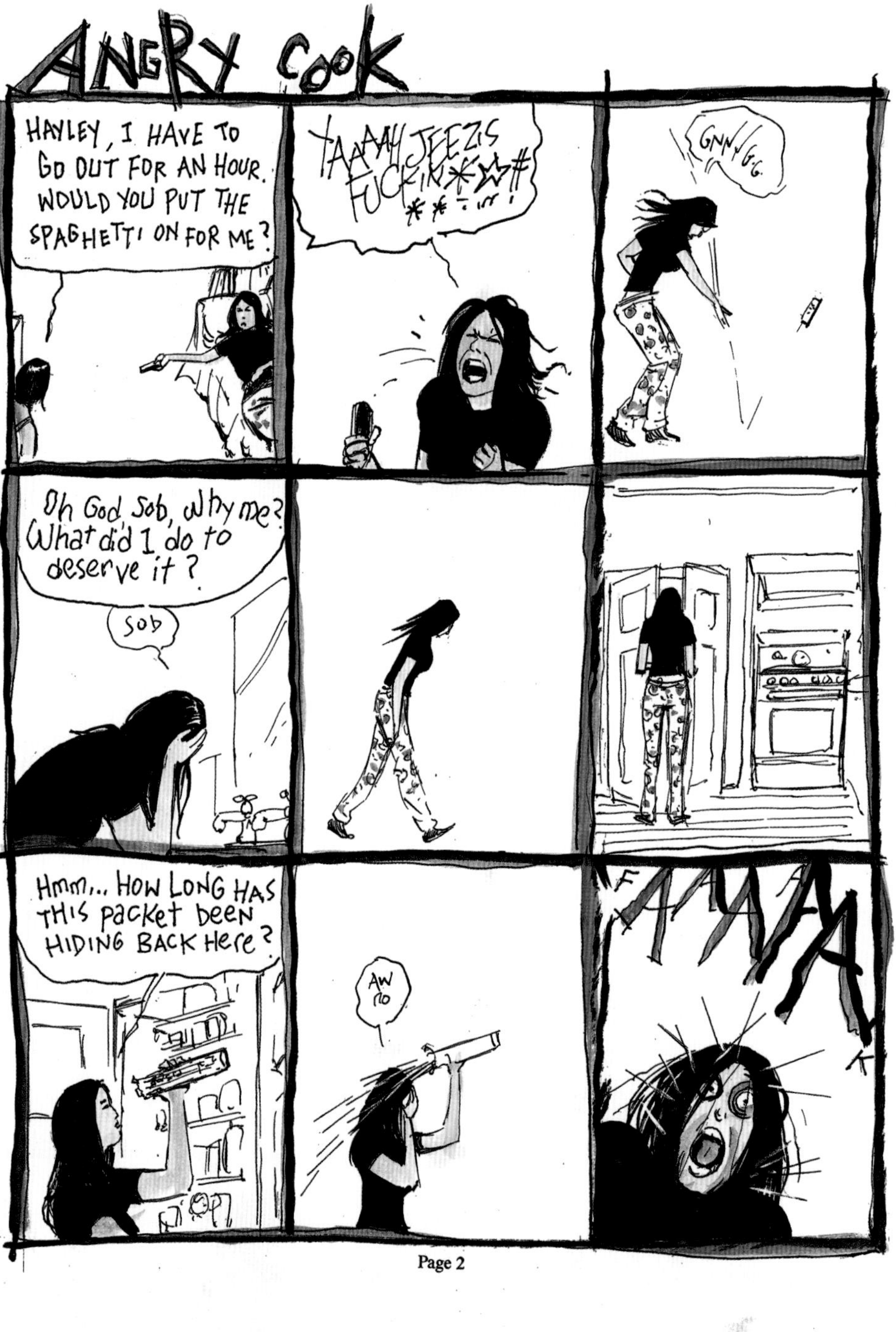
ANGRY COOK
HAYLEY, I HAVE TO GO OUT FOR AN HOUR. WOULD YOU PUT THE SPAGHETTI ON FOR ME?
TAAAAH JEEZIS FUCKIN*☆#
GNNNGG
Oh God sob, why me? What did I do to deserve it?
sob
Hmm... HOW LONG HAS THIS packet been HIDING BACK Here?
AW no
FAAAAK

Page 2

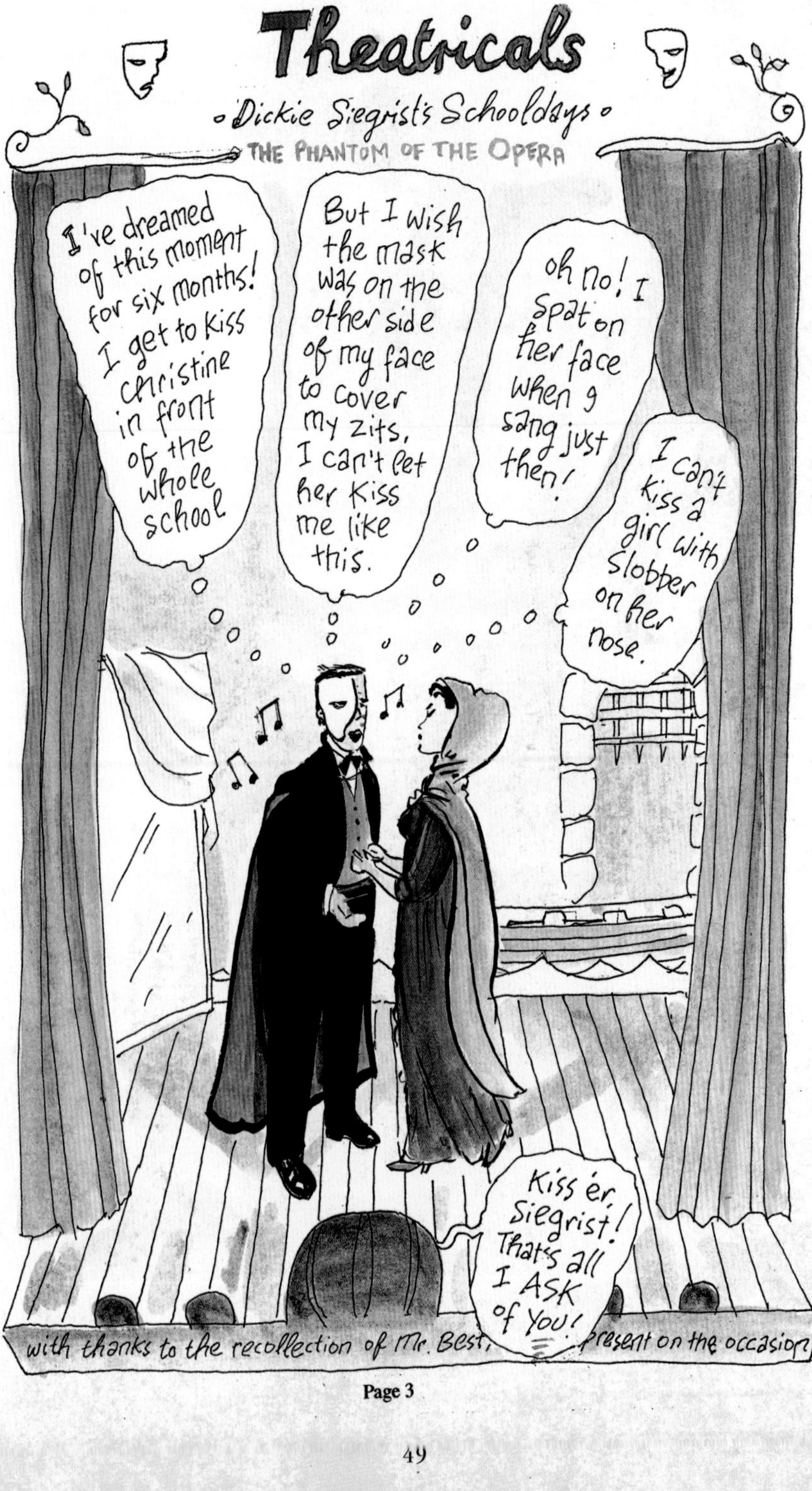
Theatricals
Dickie Siegrist's Schooldays
THE PHANTOM OF THE OPERA
I've dreamed of this moment for six months! I get to kiss Christine in front of the whole school
But I wish the mask was on the other side of my face to cover my zits. I can't let her kiss me like this.
oh no! I spat on her face when I sang just then!
I can't kiss a girl with slobber on her nose.
Kiss 'er, Siegrist! That's all I ASK of You!
with thanks to the recollection of Mr. Best, present on the occasion!

Page 3

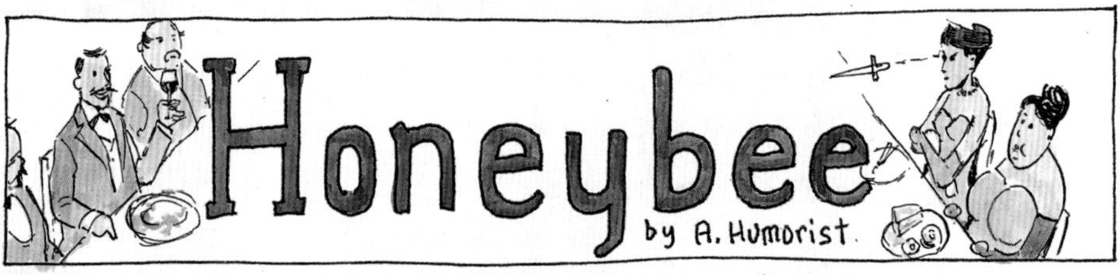
Honeybee
by A. Humorist

THE BROADWAY REVUE NOW IN ITS SECOND MONTH

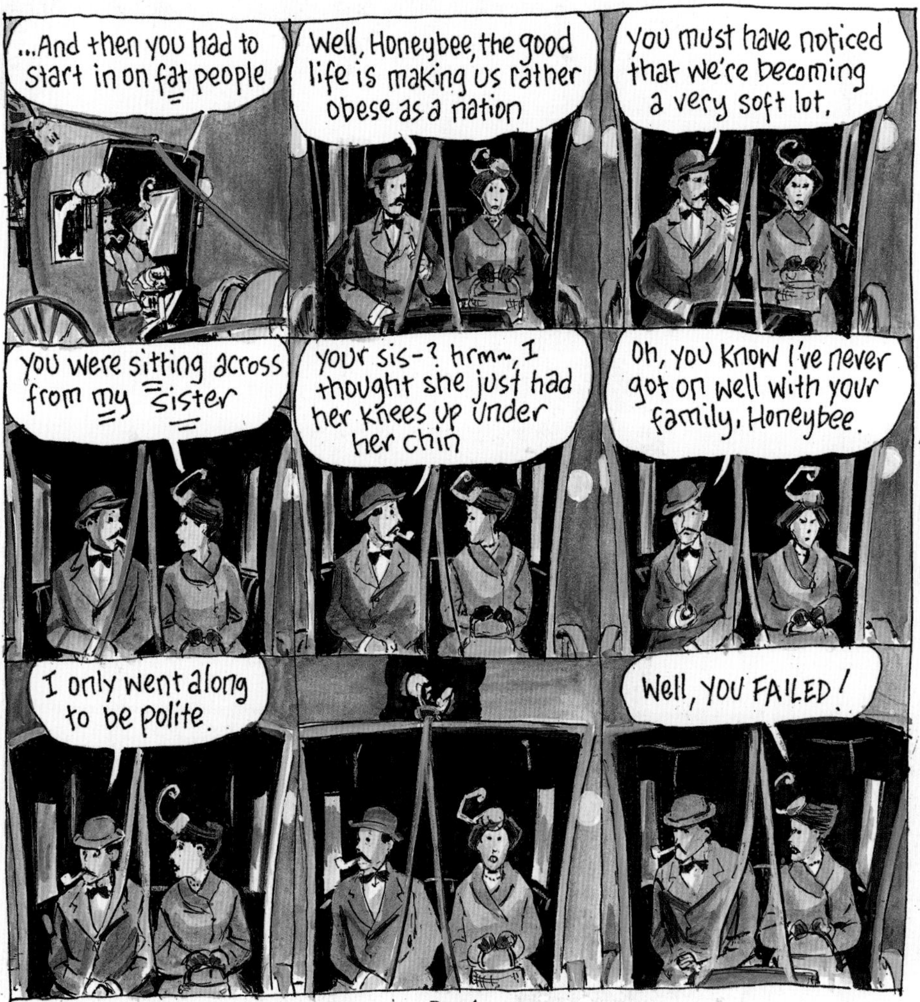
...And then you had to start in on fat people
Well, Honeybee, the good life is making us rather obese as a nation
You must have noticed that we're becoming a very soft lot.
You were sitting across from my sister
Your sis-? hrmm, I thought she just had her knees up under her chin
Oh, you know I've never got on well with your family, Honeybee.
I only went along to be polite.
Well, YOU FAILED!

Page 4

Part the Second

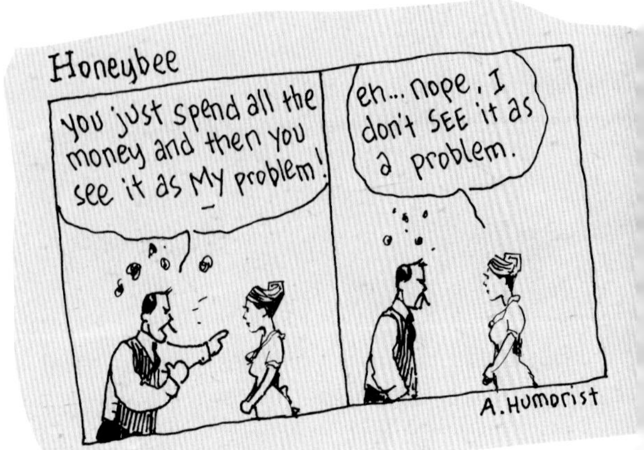
Honeybee
you just spend all the money and then you see it as My problem!
eh... nope, I don't SEE it as a problem.
A. Humorist

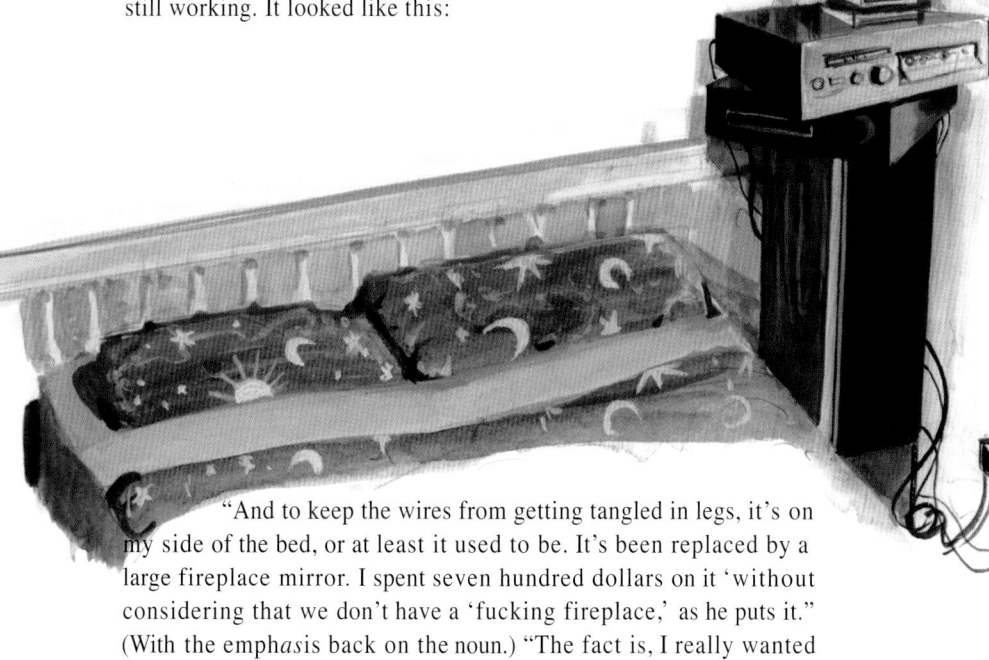

ell, it seems the wife would get annoyed with him because he had to have music playing during sex. "But don't women usually go for the romantic atmosphere." I venture. "Though for all I know he was playing death metal."

"Oh no, it wasn't for romance or for rhythm either," she said, sipping the chardonnay I hoped would tease out some intimate revelations. "He insisted he was making musicological analyses so as to delay things. You know, think about anything except sex. By the time *B*illie *H*oliday started her vocal he would already have sized up the likely personnel for the session and guessed the approximate date. He'd know that, for instance, if it was the third take of "All of Me" from 1941, he had an e x t r a - l o n g *L*ester *Y*oung sax solo to ventilate. Now, how did I remember that?"

"Are you saying you took exception to this?"

"No, what I took exception to was the bedroom CD player, or the fucking stereo," she corrected, placing the emphasis on the epithet. "Anyone else would have put their foot down at the start. It was constructed from the leftover bits from our old system that were still working. It looked like this:

"And to keep the wires from getting tangled in legs, it's on my side of the bed, or at least it used to be. It's been replaced by a large fireplace mirror. I spent seven hundred dollars on it 'without considering that we don't have a 'fucking fireplace,' as he puts it." (With the emph*a*sis back on the noun.) "The fact is, I really wanted one, and if it's useless then you can measure it against all the useless

junk *he* owns. He talked me out of it the first time I tried, so next time I picked it up on the quiet."

"Now it's in the bedroom and Dad calls it the *fucking* mirr—" She suddenly clams up. I hear the daughter arrive. How anybody could get their end away in this thoroughfare is a mystery to me.

"And if you're looking for somewhere to sit around here, the *fucking* chair's not to be confused with the *grandfather* chair, which isn't called that because of any connection with the so-called grandfather *clock*, of which we don't have one. But on account of Granddad once put his arse through it."

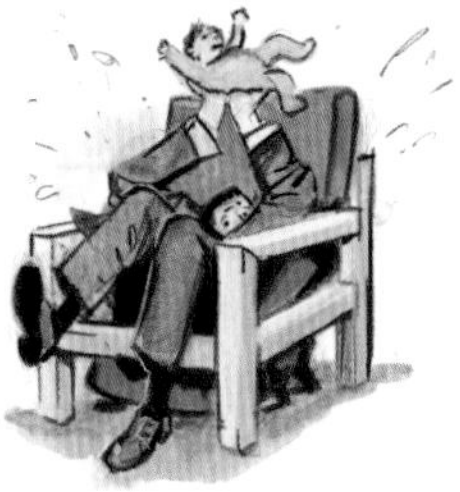

"Do you have to say 'arse'?"

"What do you mean, Mum, I just heard you say *fucking.*"

"Yes, but that's my father you're talking about."

"Regarding seats, were you home when Dad switched the toilet seats around? When you got the new system installed in the outhouse. He felt the shiny new white one should be in the bathroom. So he unscrewed them and switched them around. Then he sat on one and realized they're not interchangeable. So he had to switch them back. Spent a whole morning on the exercise. I only found out because he lost one of the screws."

"What?"

"Yes, didn't you notice one side's been held together with a paper clip for the last two years?"

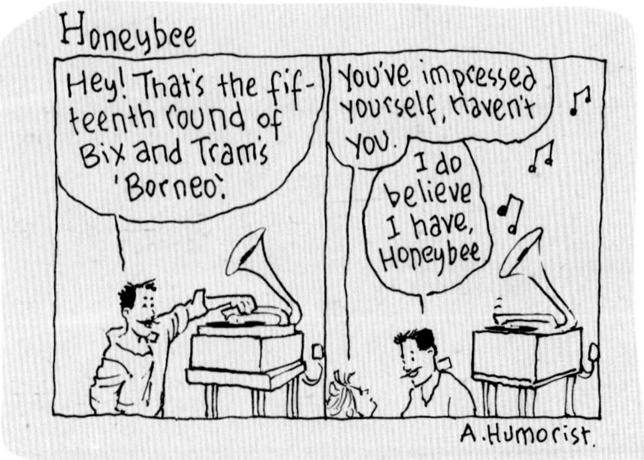
Honeybee
Hey! That's the fif-teenth round of Bix and Tram's 'Borneo'.
You've impressed yourself, haven't you.
I do believe I have, Honeybee
A.Humorist.

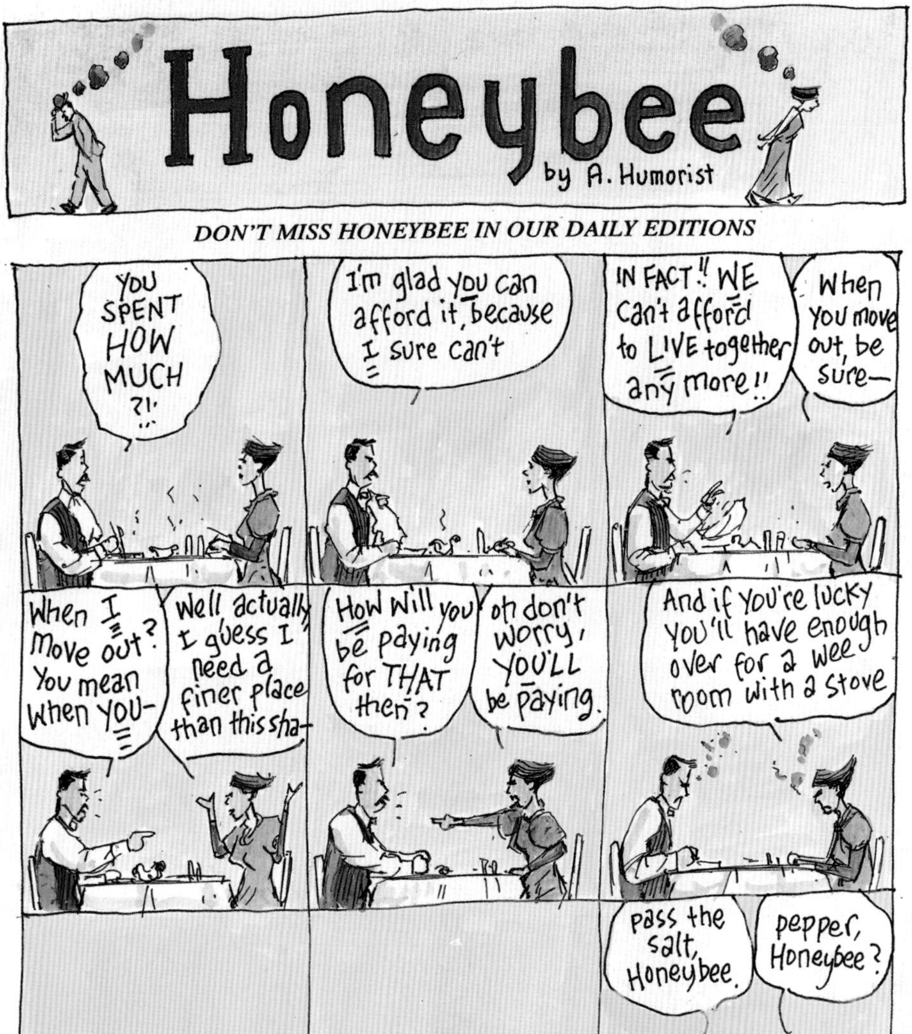
Honeybee
by A. Humorist
DON'T MISS HONEYBEE IN OUR DAILY EDITIONS
YOU SPENT HOW MUCH ?!
I'm glad you can afford it, because I sure can't
IN FACT!! WE can't afford to LIVE together any more!!
When you move out, be sure—
When I move out? You mean when YOU—
Well actually I guess I need a finer place than this sha—
How will you be paying for THAT then?
oh don't worry, YOU'LL be paying.
And if you're lucky you'll have enough over for a wee room with a stove
Pass the salt, Honeybee.
pepper, Honeybee?

Page 4

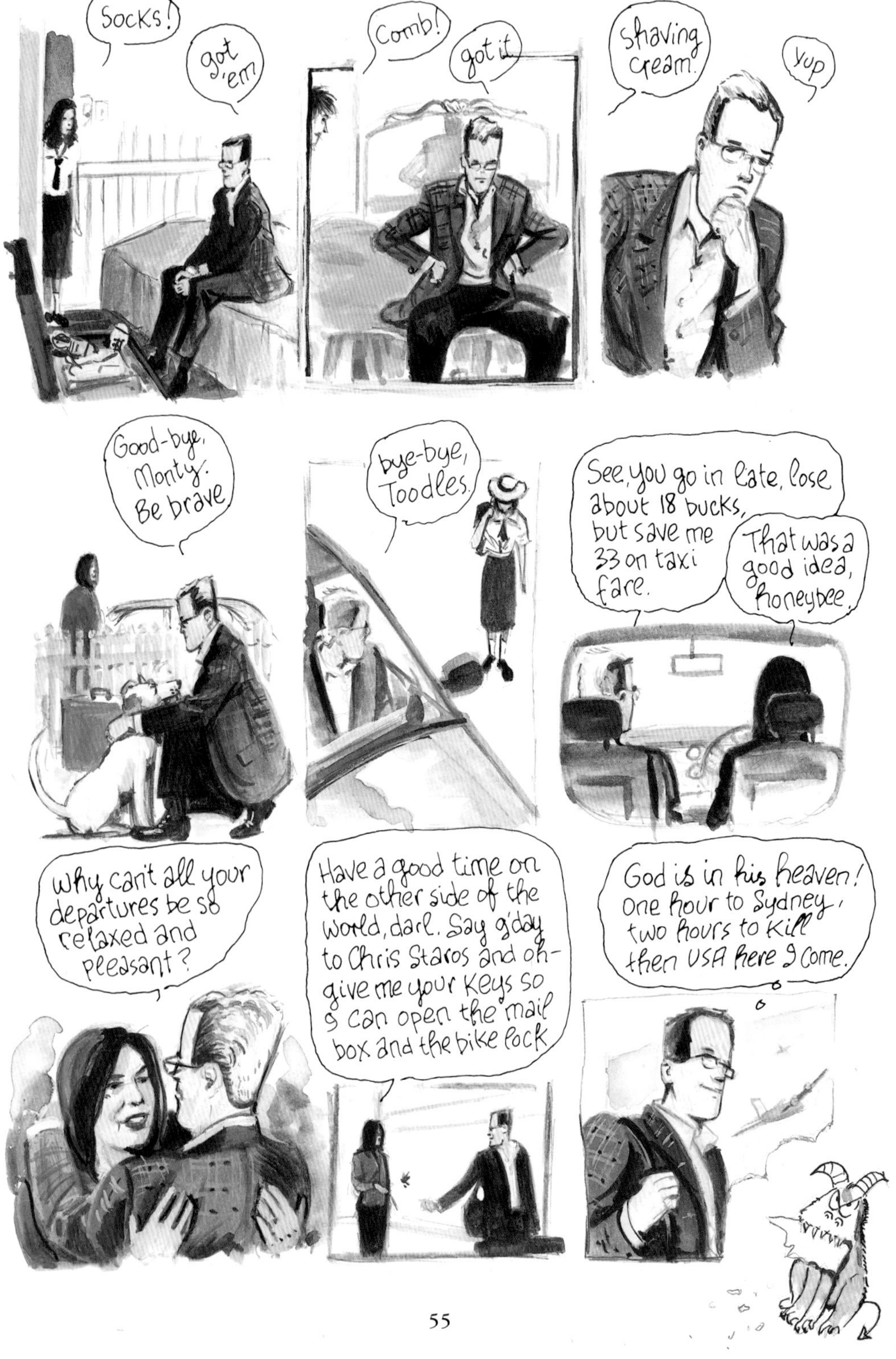
Socks!
got 'em
Comb!
got it
Shaving cream.
yup
Good-bye, Monty. Be brave
bye-bye, Toodles.
See, you go in late, lose about 18 bucks, but save me 33 on taxi fare.
That was a good idea, honeybee.
Why can't all your departures be so relaxed and pleasant?
Have a good time on the other side of the world, darl. Say g'day to Chris Staros and oh-give me your keys so I can open the mail box and the bike lock
God is in his heaven! One hour to Sydney, two hours to kill then USA here I come.

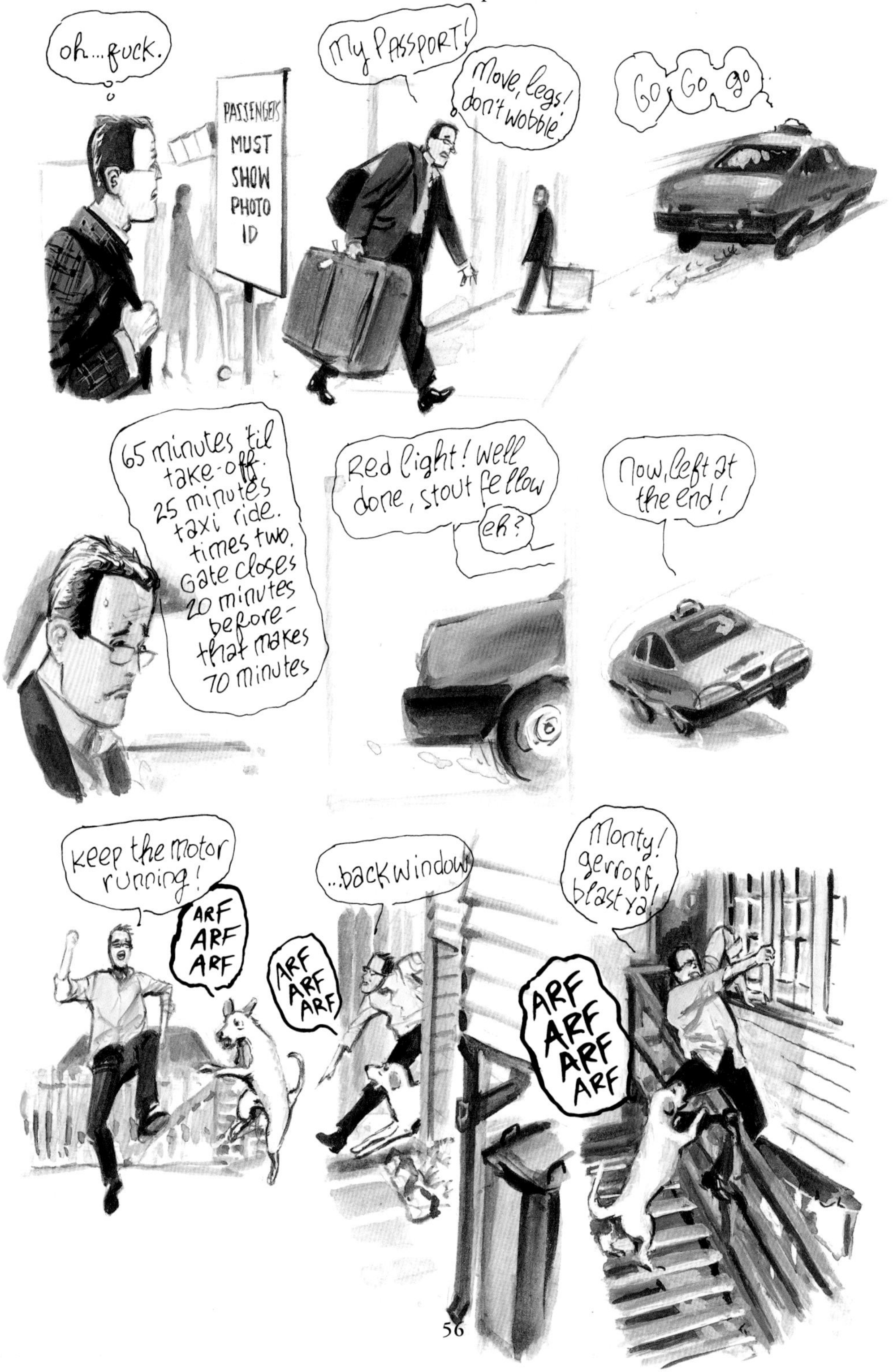
oh...fuck.
PASSENGERS MUST SHOW PHOTO ID
My PASSPORT!
Move, legs! don't wobble
Go Go go
65 minutes 'til take-off. 25 minutes taxi ride. times two. Gate closes 20 minutes before- that makes 70 minutes
Red light! Well done, stout fellow
eh?
Now, left at the end!
Keep the motor running!
ARF ARF ARF
ARF ARF ARF
...back window
Monty! gerroff blast ya!
ARF ARF ARF ARF

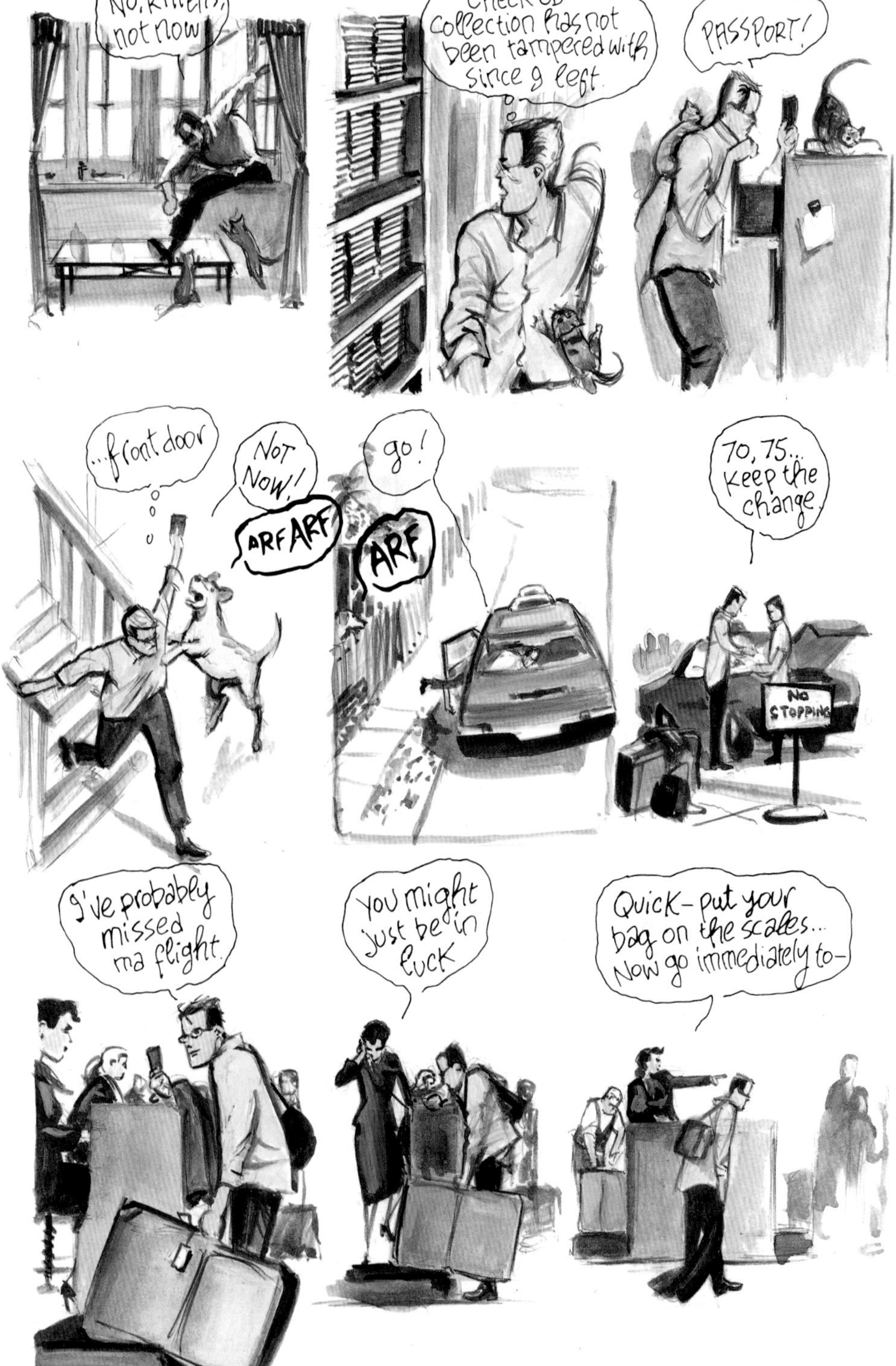
No, Kittens, not now
Check CD collection has not been tampered with since I left
PASSPORT!
...front door
NOT NOW!
ARF ARF
go!
ARF
70, 75... Keep the change.
NO STOPPING
I've probably missed ma flight.
You might just be in luck
Quick - put your bag on the scales... Now go immediately to-

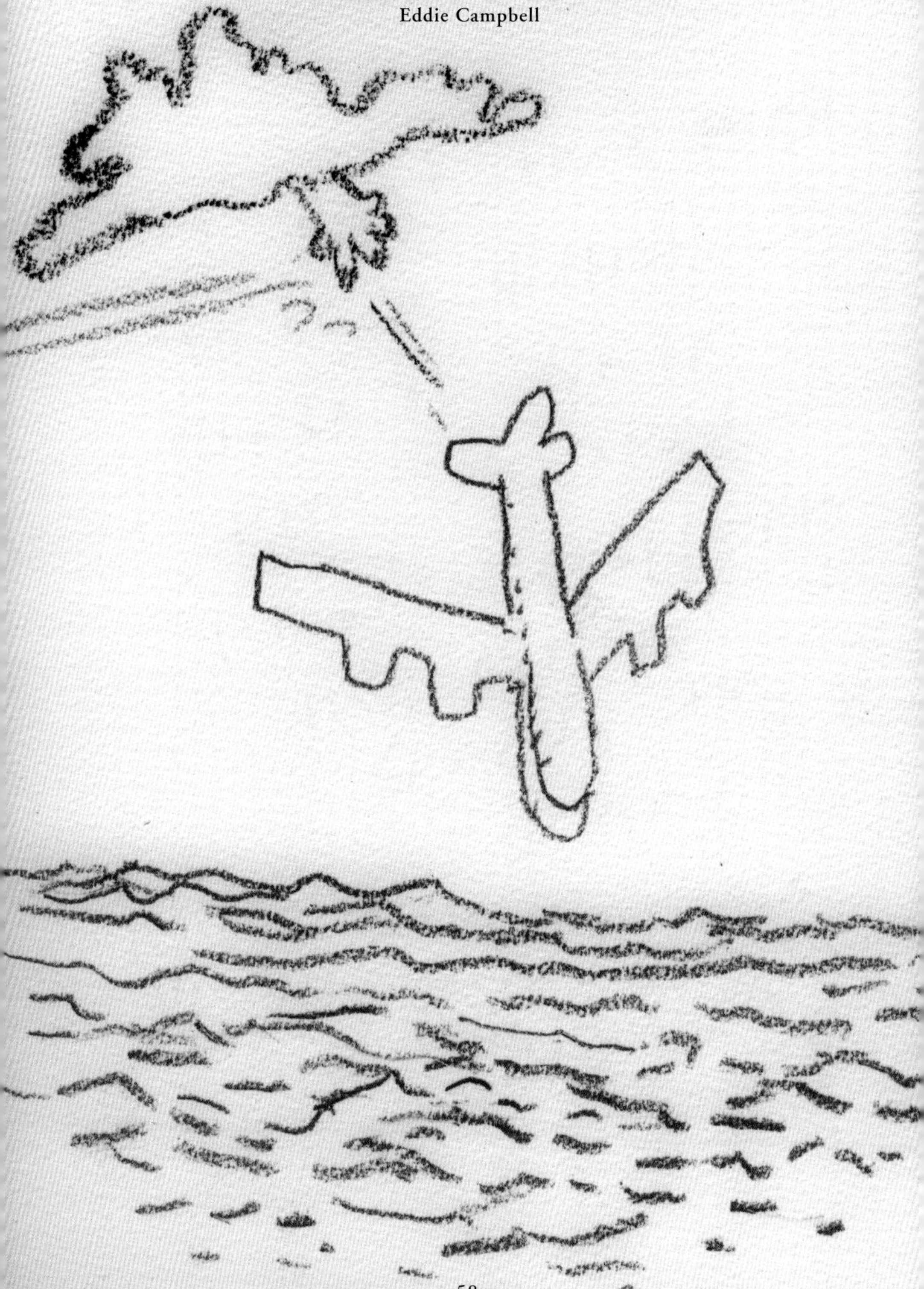

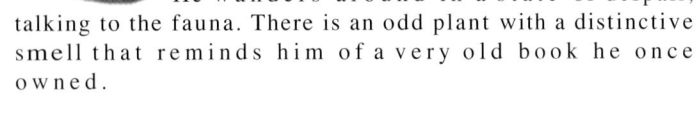

rash, **r o a r** , smash, plunge.
The artist's journey finishes with him washed
ashore on the desert island of his own mental isolation.

He wanders around in a state of despair,
talking to the fauna. There is an odd plant with a distinctive
smell that reminds him of a very old book he once
owned.

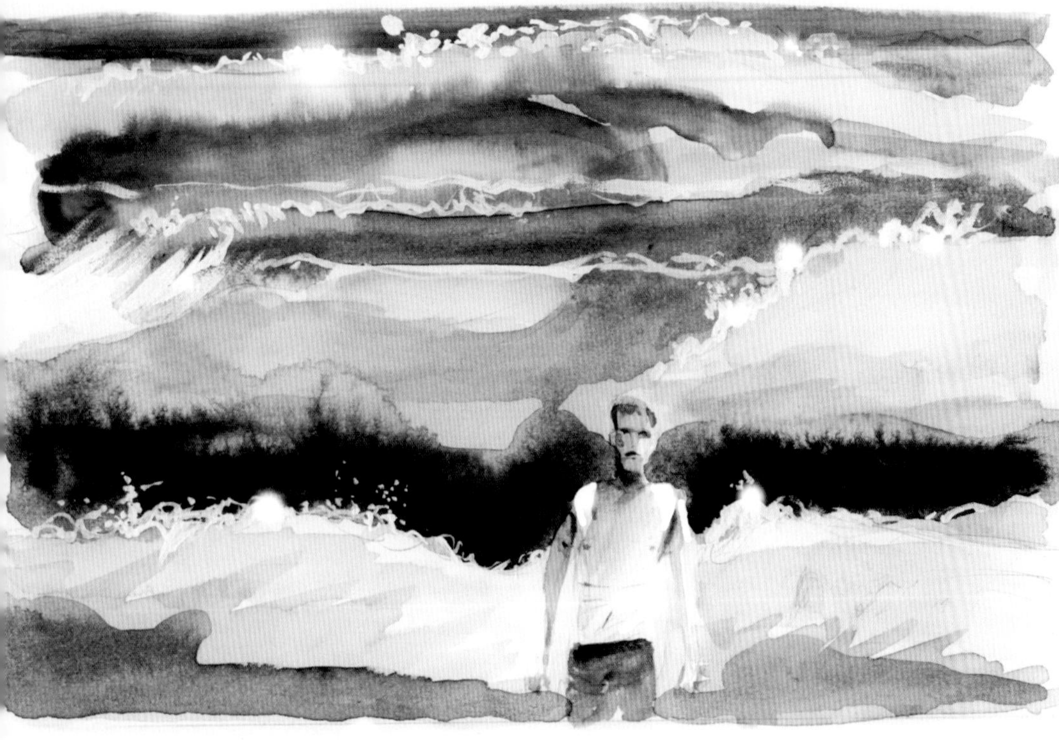

Washed ashore on the desert island.

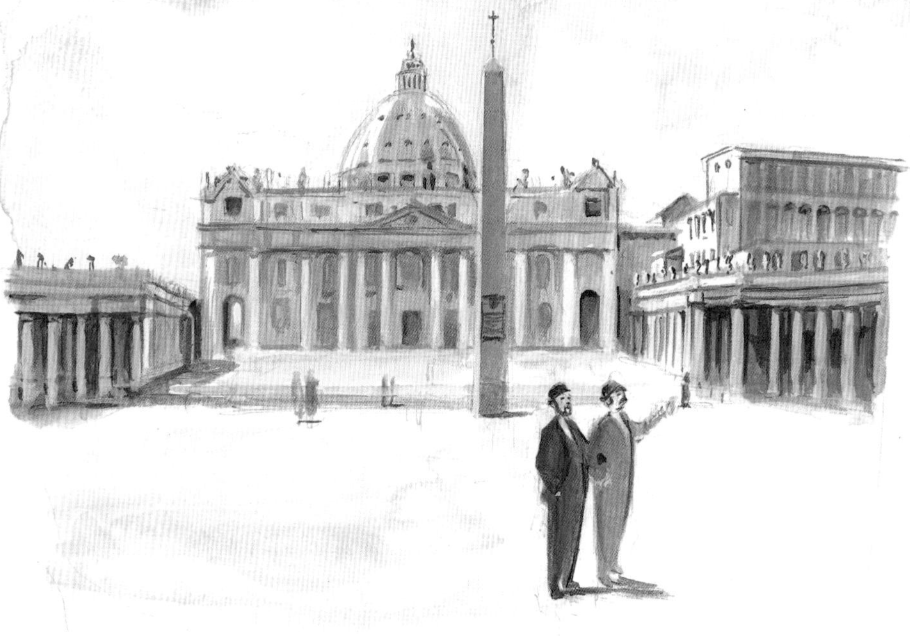

Walther Amelung, played here by our Mr. Siegrist, is cataloguing the sculptural antiquities of the Vatican in 1903.

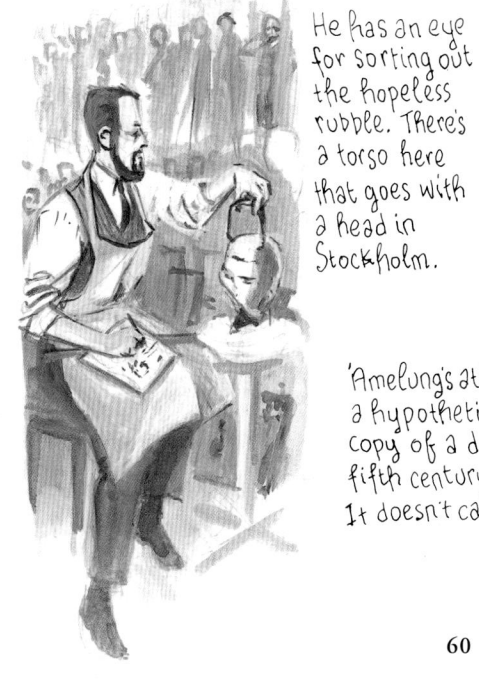

He has an eye for sorting out the hopeless rubble. There's a torso here that goes with a head in Stockholm.

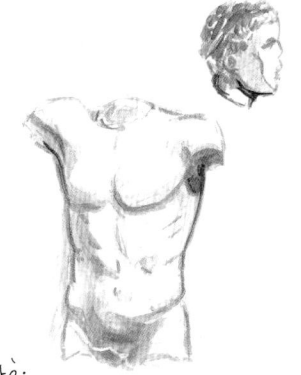

'Amelung's athletè:
a hypothetical reconstruction of a marble copy of a destroyed bronze statue, probably fifth century B.C., perhaps by Myron.
It doesn't catch on.

Or at least it doesn't catch on in the same way as Furtwangler's reconstruction of the long lost Lemnian Athena by the great Greek classical sculptor Pheidias.

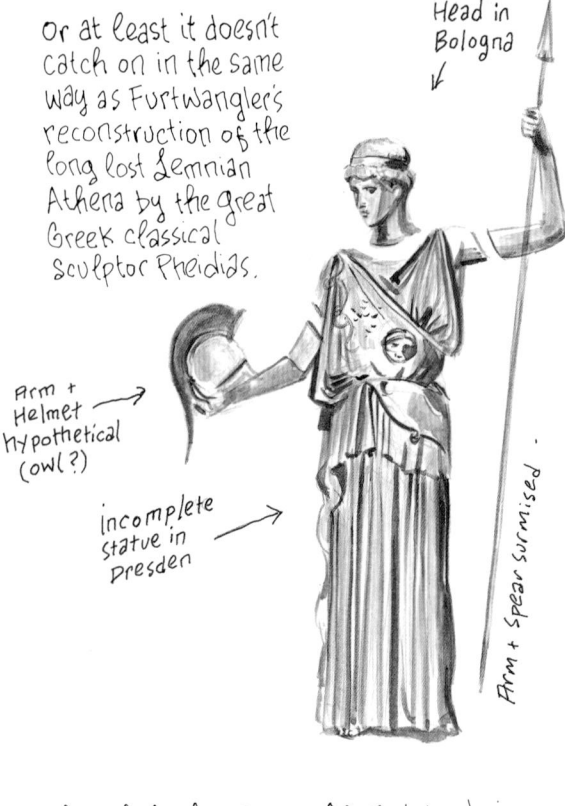

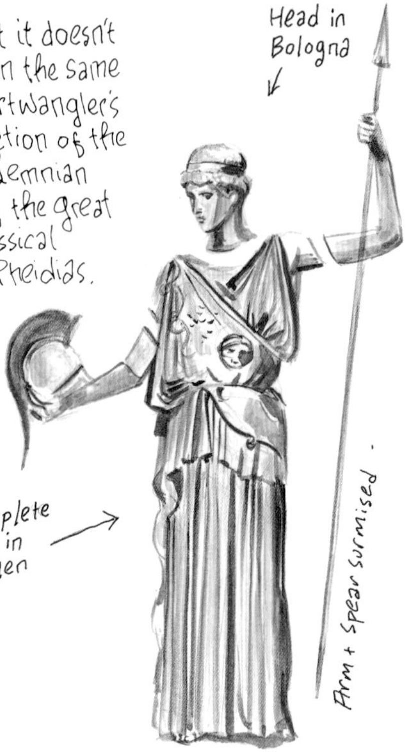
Head in Bologna
Arm + Helmet hypothetical (owl(?)
incomplete statue in Dresden
Arm + Spear surmised.

It's the cobbling together of the oeuvres of two dozen or so ancient Greek masters, all of whose works were totally destroyed centuries ago.

This kind of scholarship is out of fashion in academia:

"Amelung's willingness to limit his analyses to the concept of the artistic individual as the motivator of art has limited his legacy as an art historian."

But the scholarship of an art becomes the history of that art. We only have the concept of a "Lemnian Athena" because a couple of writers in Roman times mentioned it, and to them the only history was the account of great men.

If Furtwangler's proposed oeuvre for Pheidias is just a bunch of Frankenstein people, they're still walking about blank-eyed in text books and cast galleries.

The fictitious Pheidias does not entirely give up his seat to a real one, more unknowable and with no attributable works.

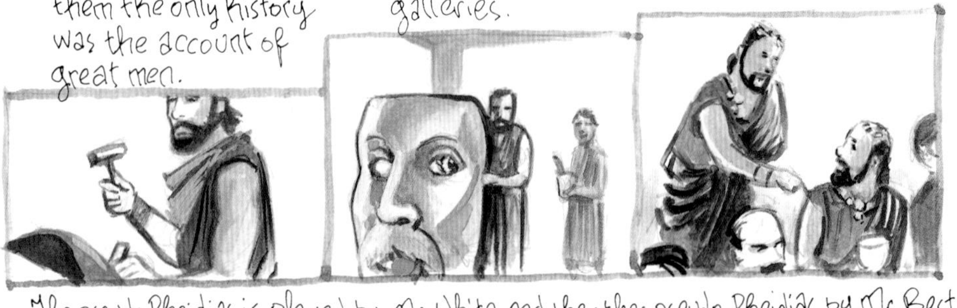

The pseudo Pheidias is played by Mr. White and the other pseudo-Pheidias by Mr. Best.

The great scholars have lovingly crafted names, like Gisela Maria Augusta Richter, Brunilde Sismondo Ridgway, Margarete Bieber, Evelyn B. Harrison, and in their books and essays they carry on endless posthumous debates, on shifting leaves, concocting their ingeniously crafted theories.

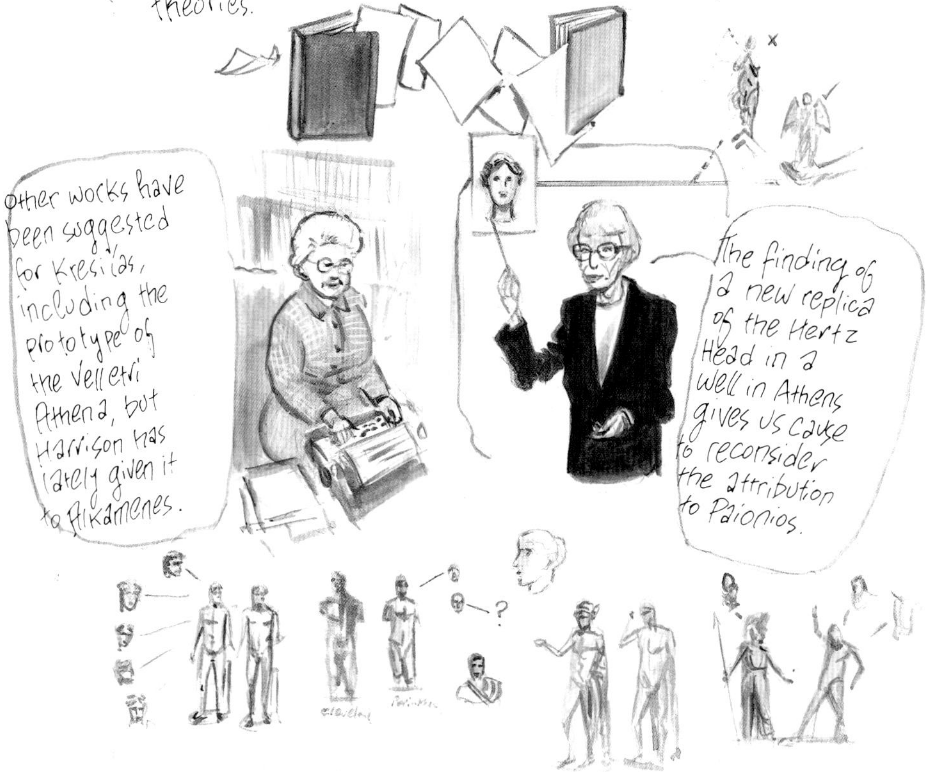
Other works have been suggested for Kresilas, including the prototype of the Velletri Athena, but Harrison has lately given it to Alkamenes.
The finding of a new replica of the Hertz Head in a well in Athens gives us cause to reconsider the attribution to Paionios.

Sometimes, dozing on his island, the artist hears them discover a new head and they're dusting its marble cranium with their tender, feathery brushes.

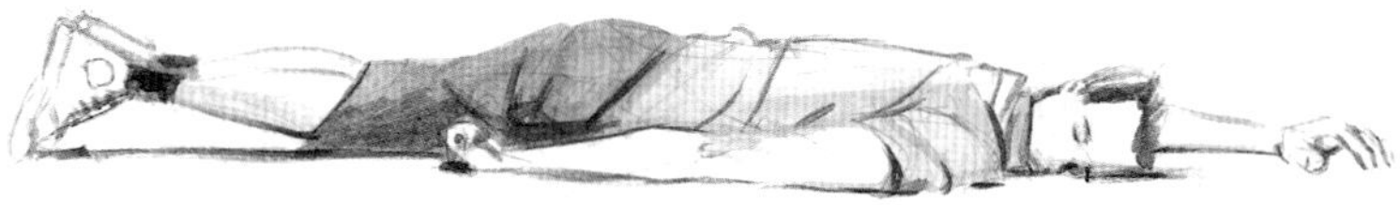

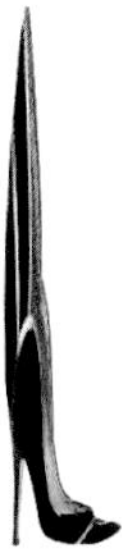

ife's a jest and all things show it.
I thought so once and now I know it."

"Rather apt, don't you think?" chuckled the art historian.

"You tell me," I answered, "you're the art historian."

"Well, to start with he's quoting the epitaph of John Gay, the eighteenth-century writer, so I shouldn't see it as a clue to our fellow having done away with himself or anything like that. His prevailing theme was the chaos behind the facade; the upending disruption."

"He seems to have collected Xeroxes of humor in art, literature, and any other type, from the beginning of civilization." I can't get those plastic bags full of stuff out of my noodle, which is where I picked up the quote, carefully noted on the intro sheet of one volume.

"And that isn't easy, you know. There isn't a lot of it. The ancients stuck it up on the fridge much like we do, until it disintegrated and fell off. What interested him was the idea that when we appreciate a joke across the centuries, time may appear to fall away, and we can create the illusion, and we must never forget that it is but an illusion, of communicating with the past. For instance, to understand *E*rasmus of *R*otterdam you'd need to know a great deal about the time in which he lived, but if you look at one of his marginal doodles, well that could have been drawn yesterday instead of five hundred years ago. There's a common notion that humor dates quickly and becomes obscure, but the opposite can be the case. Nevertheless, where do you go and what do you do after you've laughed at the futility of the universe? That's the question I think you have to answer before you find your 'Rosebud,' Mr. Detective."

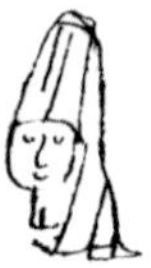

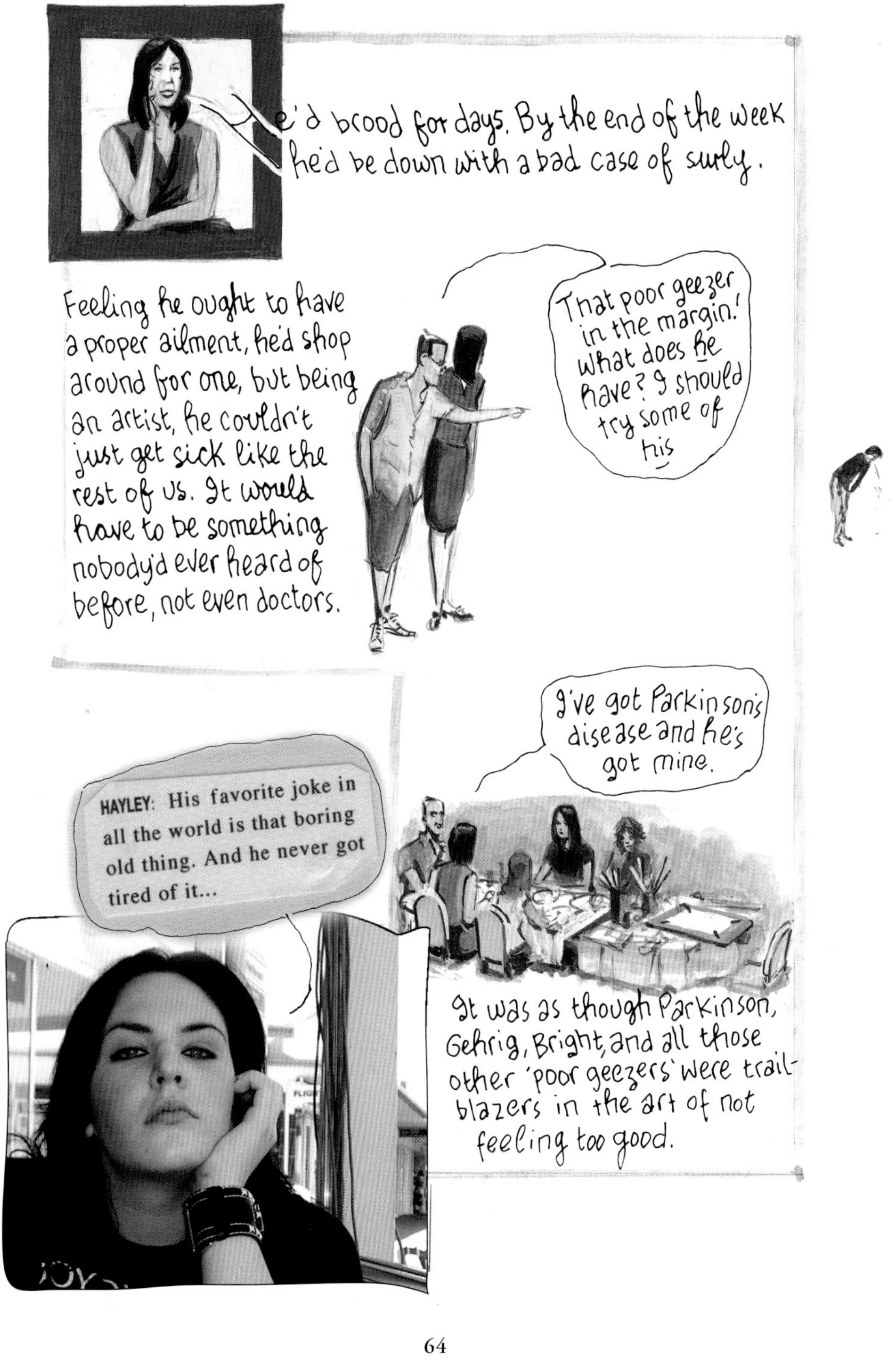
He'd brood for days. By the end of the week he'd be down with a bad case of surly.
Feeling he ought to have a proper ailment, he'd shop around for one, but being an artist, he couldn't just get sick like the rest of us. It would have to be something nobody'd ever heard of before, not even doctors.
That poor geezer in the margin! What does he have? I should try some of his
I've got Parkinson's disease and he's got mine.
It was as though Parkinson, Gehrig, Bright, and all those other 'poor geezers' were trail-blazers in the art of not feeling too good.
HAYLEY: His favorite joke in all the world is that boring old thing. And he never got tired of it...

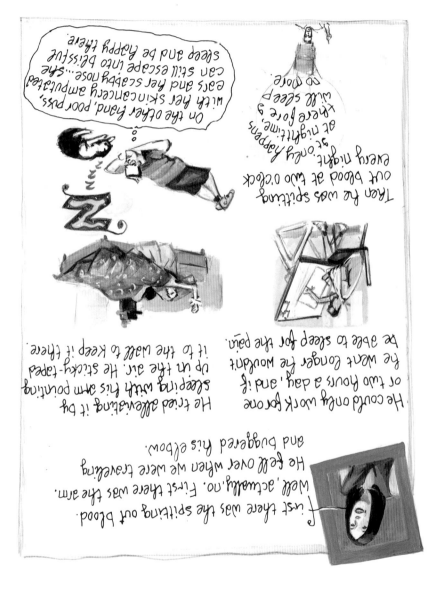

First there was the spitting out blood. Well, actually, no. First there was the arm. He fell over when we were traveling and buggered his elbow.

He could only work for one or two hours a day, and if he went longer he wouldn't be able to sleep for the pain.

He tried alleviating it by sleeping with his arm pointing up in the air. He sticky-taped it to the wall to keep it there.

Then he was spitting out blood at two o'clock every night. It only happens at night time; there fore he will sleep no more.

On the other hand, poor puss, with her skincancery amputated ears and her scabby nose...she can still escape into blissful sleep and be happy there

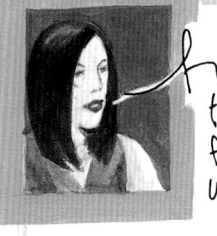

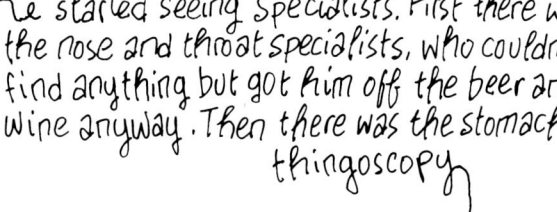

He started seeing specialists. First there were the nose and throat specialists, who couldn't find anything but got him off the beer and wine anyway. Then there was the stomach thingoscopy

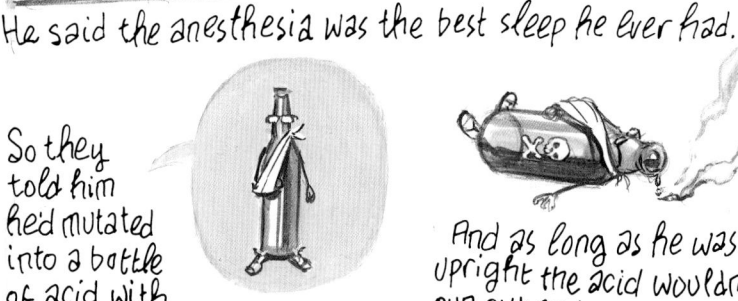

He said the anesthesia was the best sleep he ever had.

So they told him he'd mutated into a bottle of acid with no stopper.

And as long as he was upright the acid wouldn't run out and burn a hole in him.

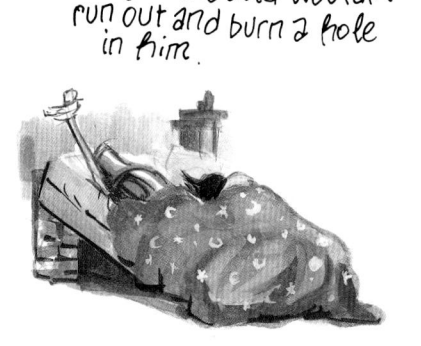

Now we have bricks under one end of the bed.

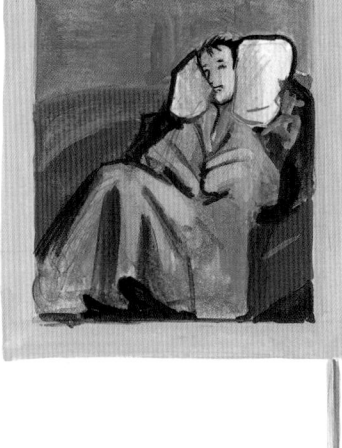

In the end he rigged up a bean bag on the chaise longue, until I got him to a specialist who told him what he wanted to hear.

I can tell just by looking at you, there's nothing wrong with your stomach.

I want you off the losec and back on the guinness

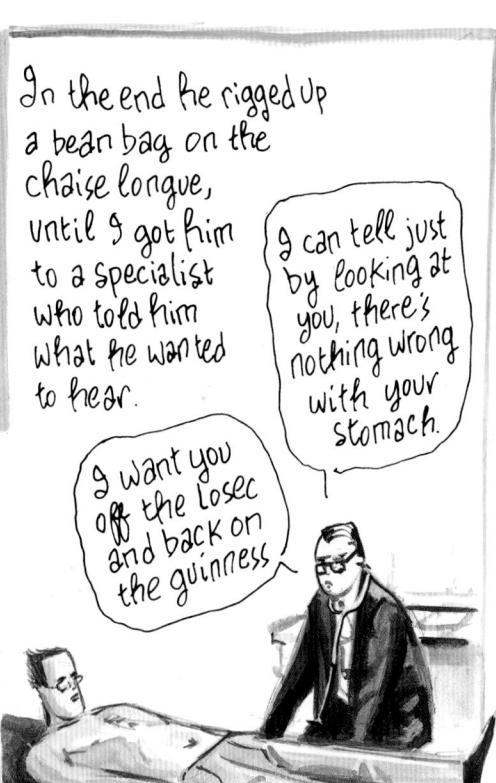

'Campbell's Complaint' (whatever it might be) remains uncatalogued by medical science.

Honeybee

I've got Campbell's disease and he's got mine.

And a right pair of boobs you both are.

A. Humorist

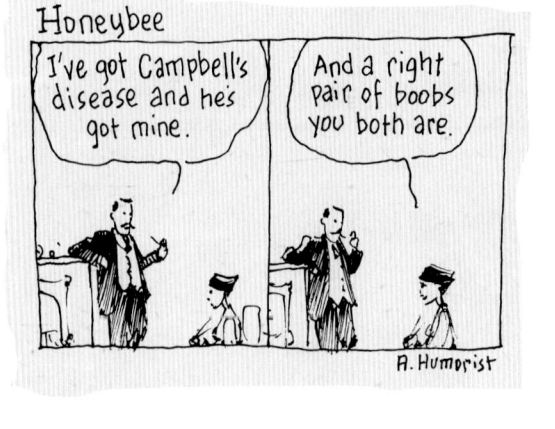

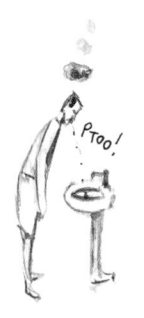

Proo!

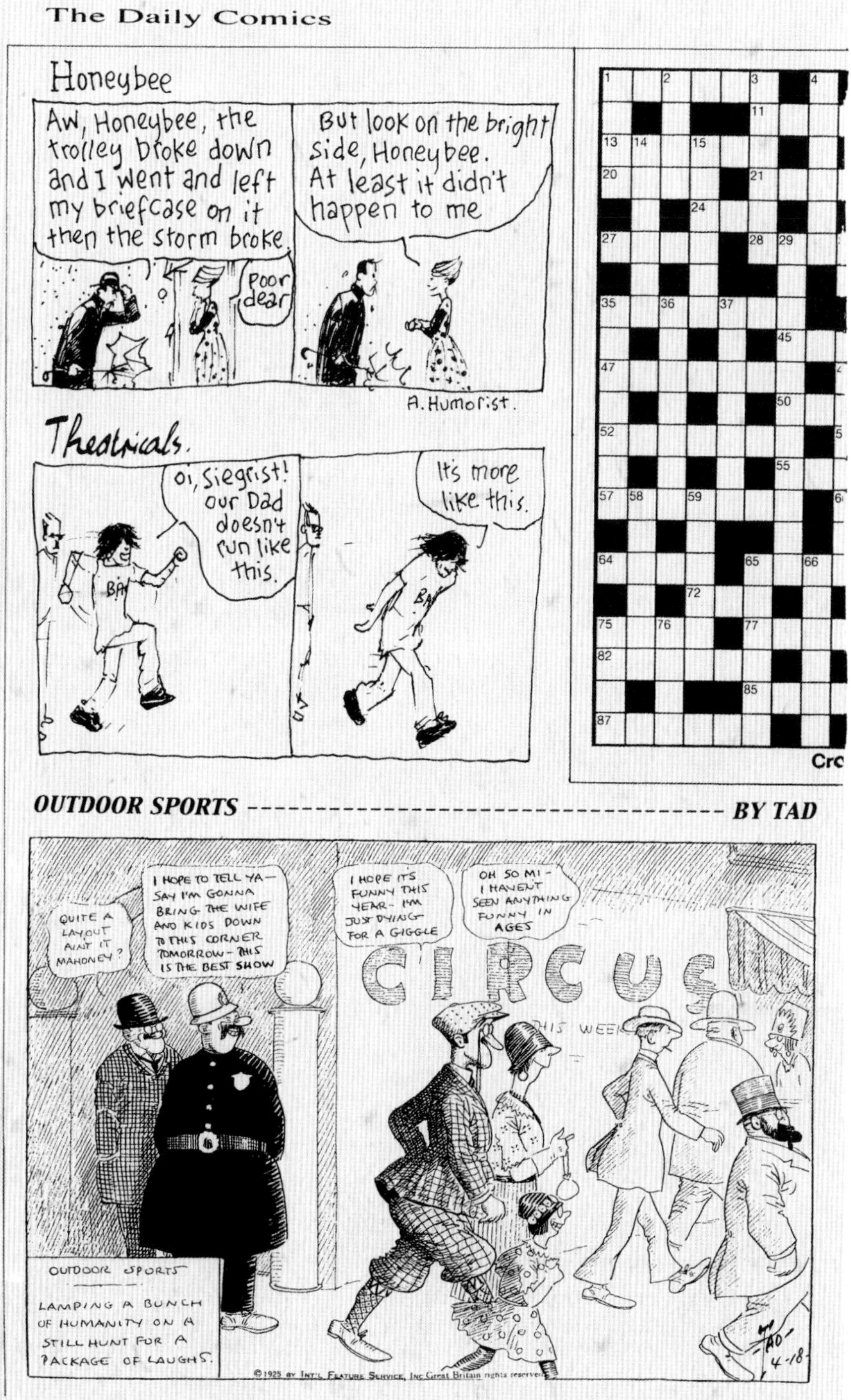
The Daily Comics
Honeybee
Aw, Honeybee, the trolley broke down and I went and left my briefcase on it then the storm broke.
Poor dear
But look on the bright side, Honeybee. At least it didn't happen to me
A. Humorist.
Theatricals.
Oi, Siegrist! our Dad doesn't run like this.
It's more like this.
Cro
OUTDOOR SPORTS ---------------------------------- BY TAD
QUITE A LAYOUT AINT IT MAHONEY?
I HOPE TO TELL YA— SAY I'M GONNA BRING THE WIFE AND KIDS DOWN TO THIS CORNER TOMORROW— THIS IS THE BEST SHOW
I HOPE ITS FUNNY THIS YEAR— I'M JUST DYING FOR A GIGGLE
OH SO MI— I HAVENT SEEN ANYTHING FUNNY IN AGES
CIRCUS
OUTDOOR SPORTS
LAMPING A BUNCH OF HUMANITY ON A STILL HUNT FOR A PACKAGE OF LAUGHS.
TAD 4-18
©1925 BY INT'L FEATURE SERVICE, INC Great Britain rights reserved

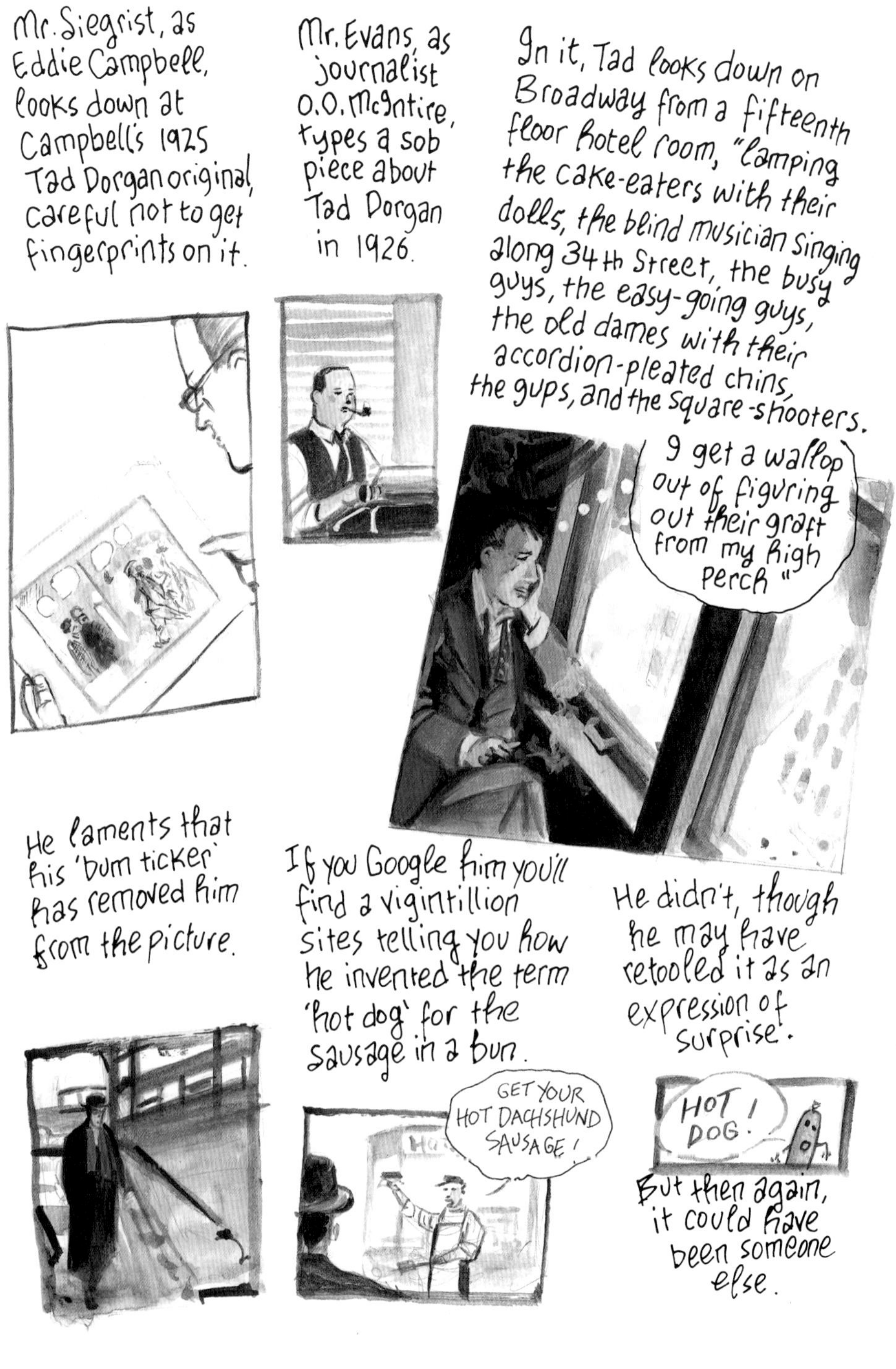
Mr. Siegrist, as Eddie Campbell, looks down at Campbell's 1925 Tad Dorgan original, careful not to get fingerprints on it.
Mr. Evans, as journalist O.O. McIntire, types a sob piece about Tad Dorgan in 1926.
In it, Tad looks down on Broadway from a fifteenth floor hotel room, "lamping the cake-eaters with their dolls, the blind musician singing along 34th Street, the busy guys, the easy-going guys, the old dames with their accordion-pleated chins, the gups, and the square-shooters.
I get a wallop out of figuring out their graft from my high perch"
He laments that his 'bum ticker' has removed him from the picture.
If you Google him you'll find a vigintillion sites telling you how he invented the term 'hot dog' for the sausage in a bun.
GET YOUR HOT DACHSHUND SAUSAGE!
He didn't, though he may have retooled it as an expression of surprise.
HOT! DOG!
But then again, it could have been someone else.

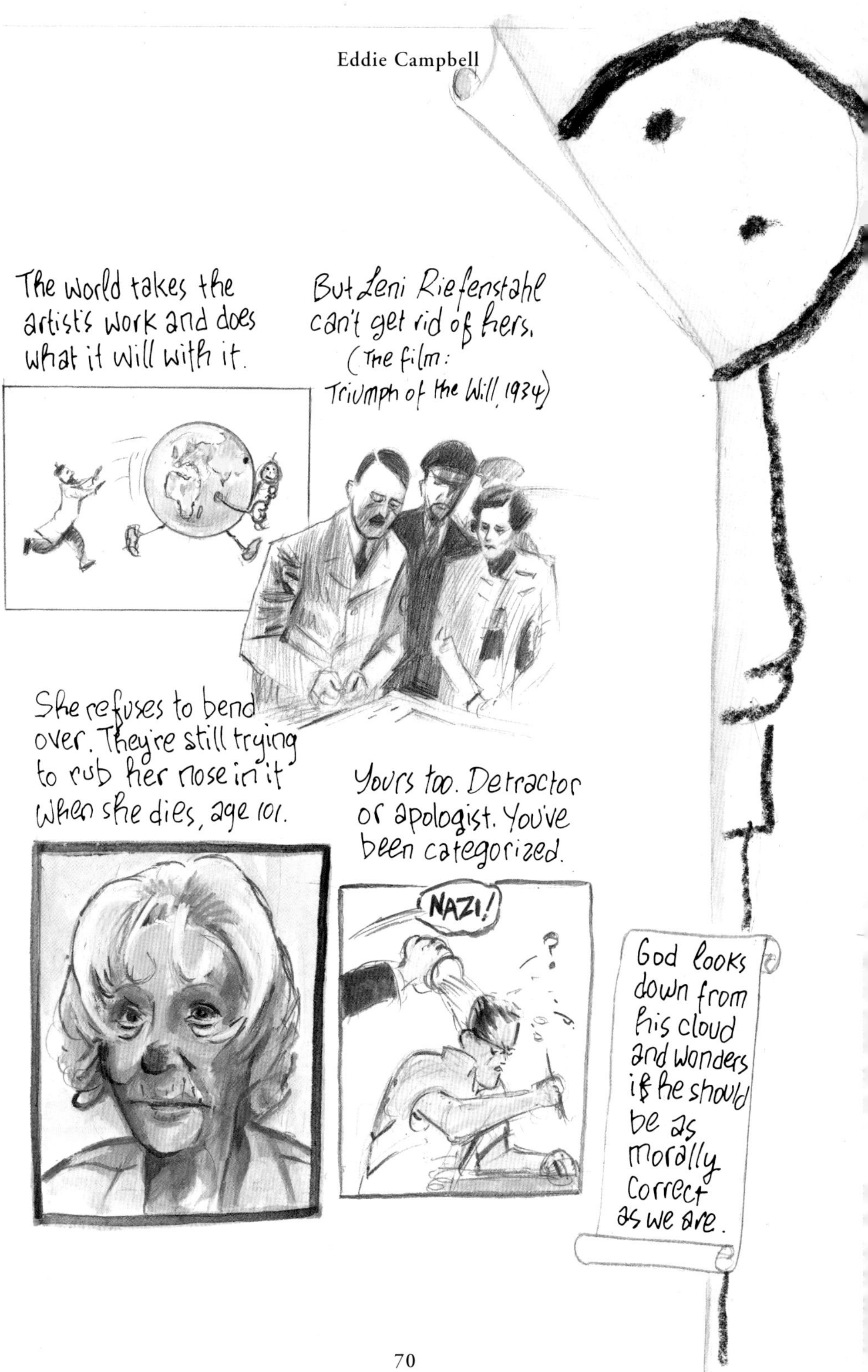
The world takes the artist's work and does what it will with it.
But Leni Riefenstahl can't get rid of hers.
(The film: Triumph of the Will, 1934)
She refuses to bend over. They're still trying to rub her nose in it when she dies, age 101.
Yours too. Detractor or apologist. You've been categorized.
NAZI!
God looks down from his cloud and wonders if he should be as morally correct as we are.

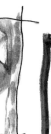

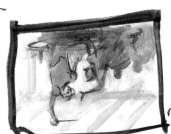

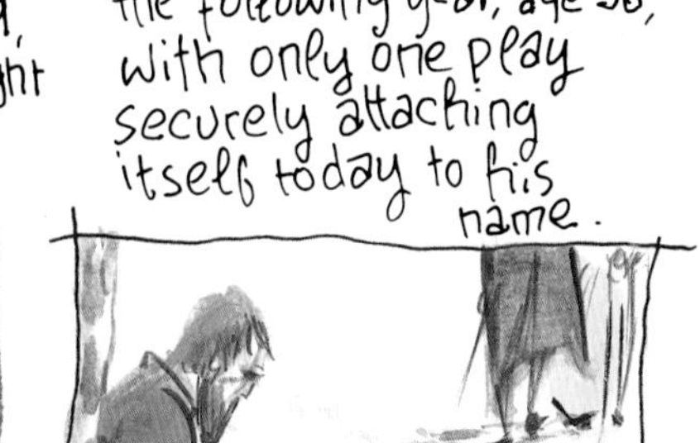

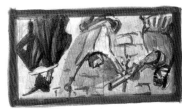

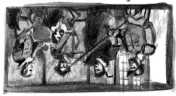

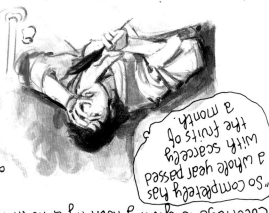

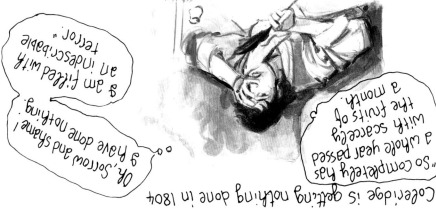

Coleridge is getting nothing done in 1804
"So completely has a whole year passed with scarcely the fruits of a month.
Oh, Sorrow and shame! I have done nothing.
I am filled with an indescribable terror."

In older days, writers had more urgent things to worry about. Kyd is arrested in 1593 under suspicion of libel.

In his lodgings, a heretical tract is found. He attributes it, under torture, to Marlowe.

Marlowe is stabbed to death in a tavern, age 29, before he can be brought before the authorities.

Kyd dies in poverty, the following year, age 36, with only one play securely attaching itself today to his name.

Nashe and Jonson put on a play in 1597 that is so thoroughly suppressed that we may never know what it was about.

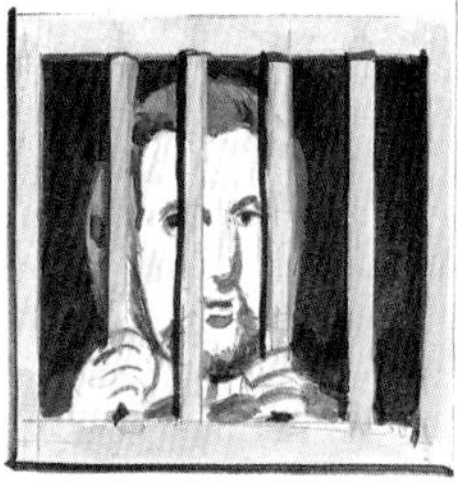

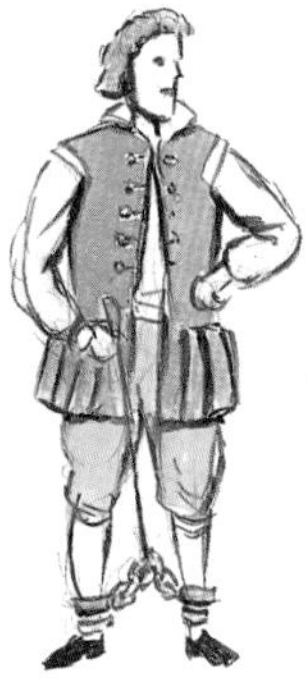

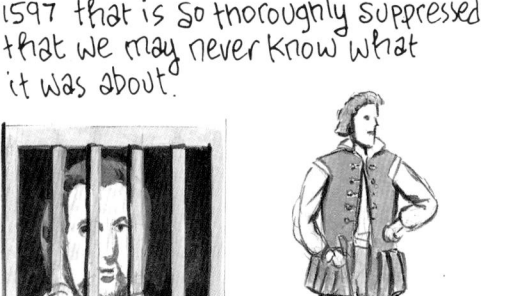

Shakespeare, contemporary of all these fellows, keeps his nose clean, writes around two plays a year for twenty years, then retires in comfort.

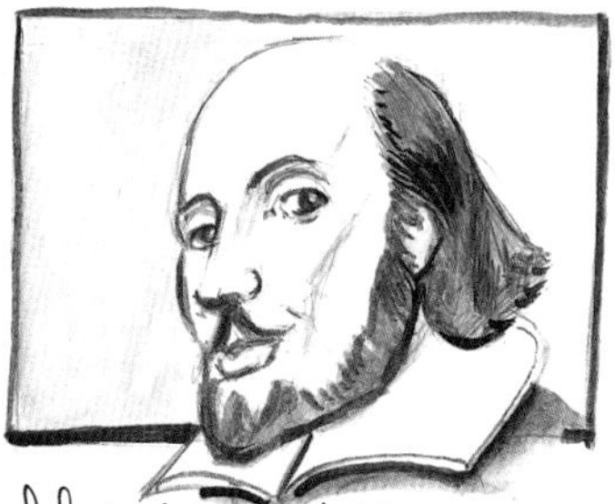

Meanwhile...
Funnyman Will Kempe leaves us a pamphlet from 1600, being an account of his morris dance from London to Norwich

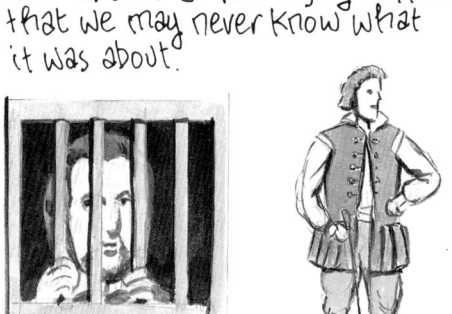

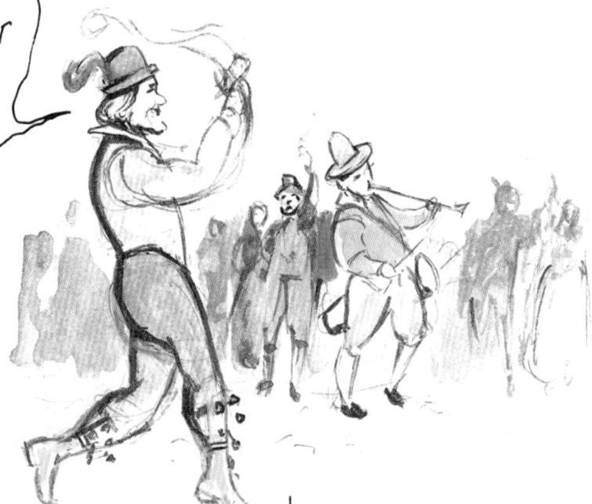
I, cavaliero Kemp, head-master of morris-dancers, high head borough of heighs and onely tricker of your trill-lillies and best bel-shangles between Sion and Mount Surrey, began frolickely to foote it.

Let us take this opportunity to give credit to our dependable troupe of players, particularly Mr. Siegrist for recreating Nashe in leg irons from the modest woodcut which is the only known image of that writer and, playing Kempe, "Dazzlin'" White, who disdains to allow us to use the antiquated "Mr.," so prevalent elsewhere in these notations.

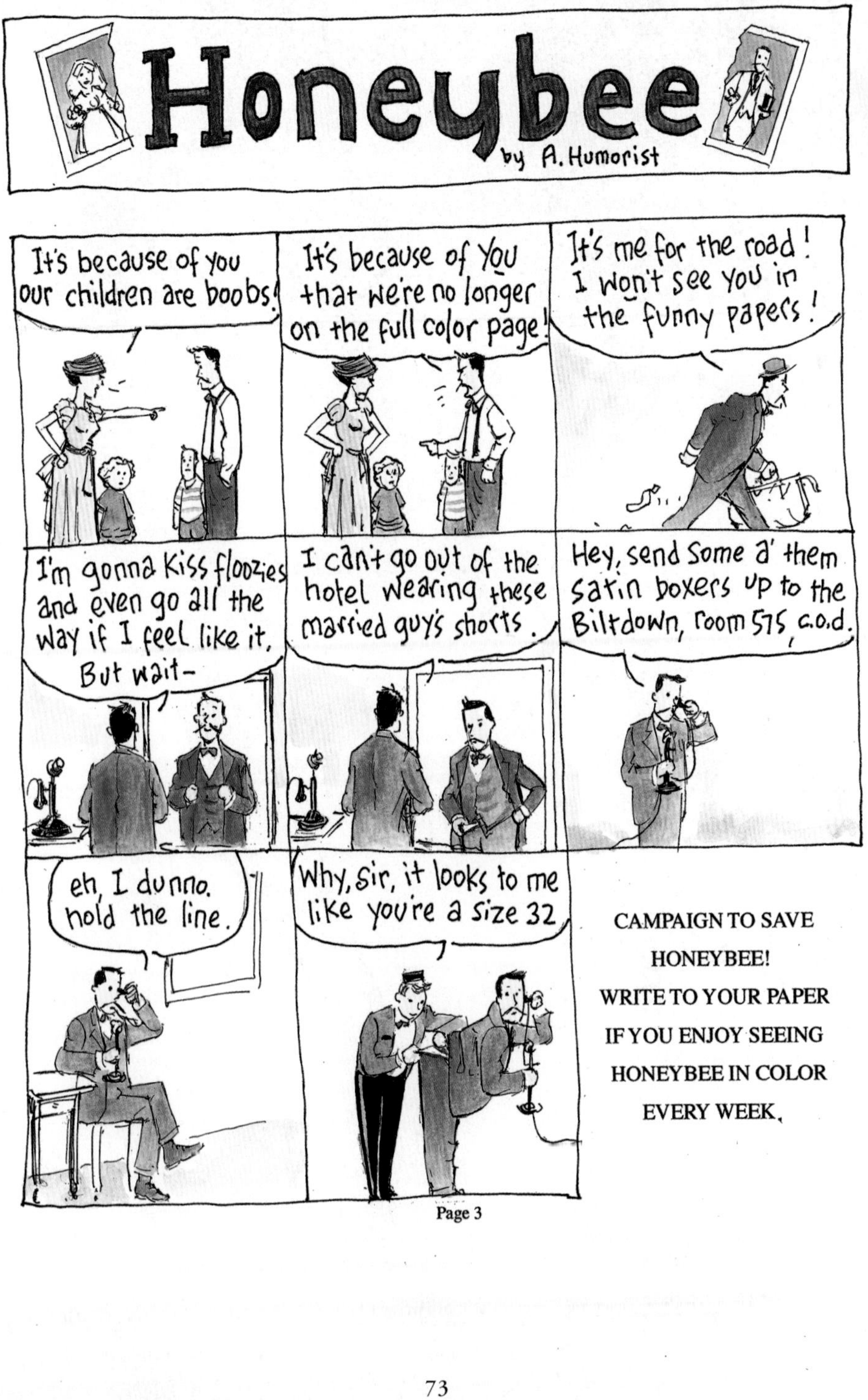
Honeybee
by A. Humorist
It's because of you our children are boobs!
It's because of you that we're no longer on the full color page!
It's me for the road! I won't see you in the funny papers!
I'm gonna kiss floozies and even go all the way if I feel like it, But wait–
I can't go out of the hotel wearing these married guy's shorts.
Hey, send some a' them satin boxers up to the Biltdown, room 575, c.o.d.
eh, I dunno. hold the line.
Why, sir, it looks to me like you're a size 32
CAMPAIGN TO SAVE HONEYBEE! WRITE TO YOUR PAPER IF YOU ENJOY SEEING HONEYBEE IN COLOR EVERY WEEK.
Page 3

Him and cats and dogs. That's not counting all his imaginary people. You've got to remember that when you're talking about artists. His personal space was a thriving community of them ...

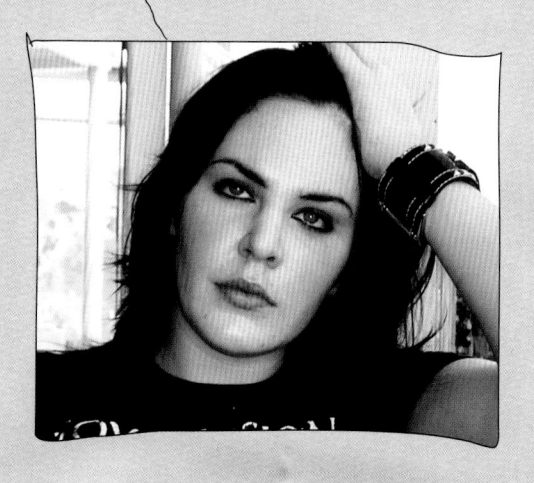

Bix Beiderbecke would be in there. It was during the period when he had constant DTs and was looking for Mexicans under the bed.

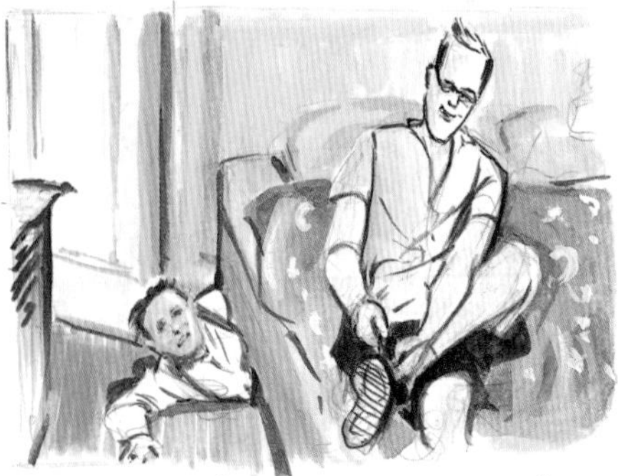

He'd be exchanging surreal quips with Hoagy Carmichael if he was there too.

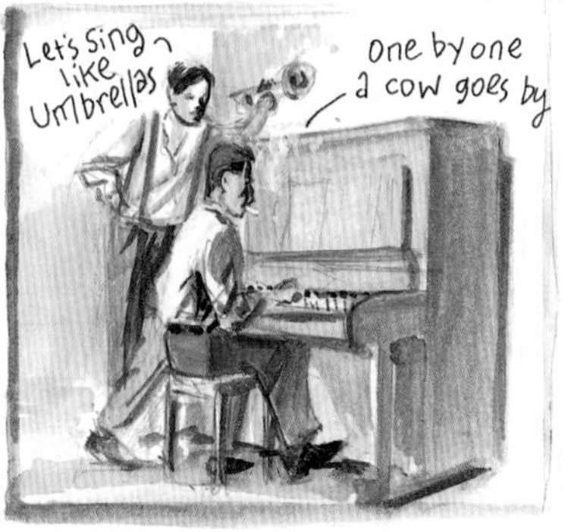
Let's sing like umbrellas
One by one a cow goes by

Eckard would be duetting with Punto, the horn virtuoso who wrote a funny minuet with a punctuating bass plunge that could only put one in mind of a fart.

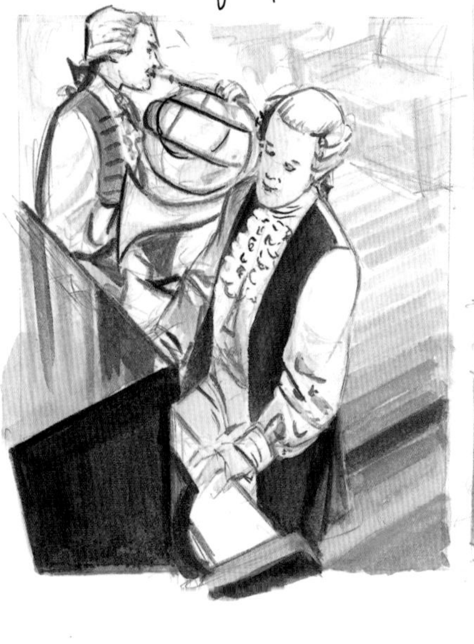

He got on well with Hoagy. Took a cadenza on *Manhattan Rag*. Those 18th century guys knew how to improvise.

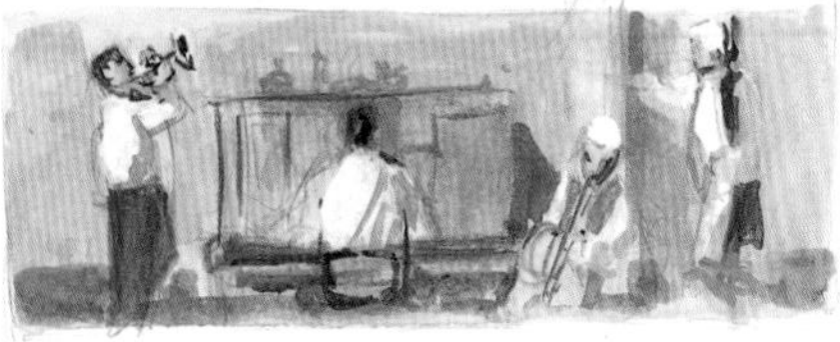

Eckard and Dad are both Mr. Siegrist, so you don't see them in the same panel.

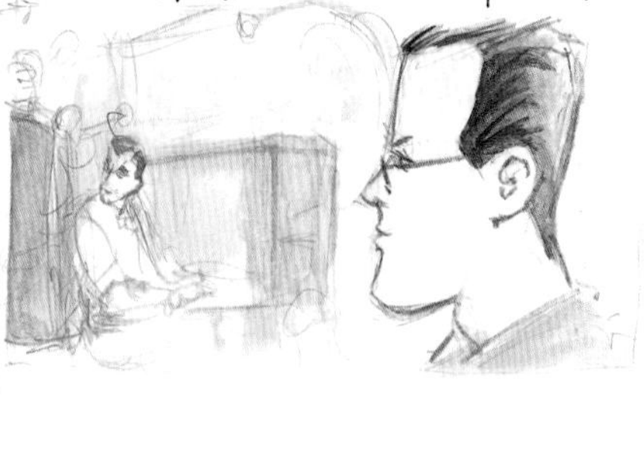

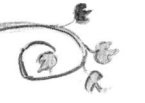**I**ke and Mike are here too, named by Dad after a Rube Goldberg comic. This same pair of rabbits appears many times in the margins of two separate illuminated Gothic manuscripts ⇨

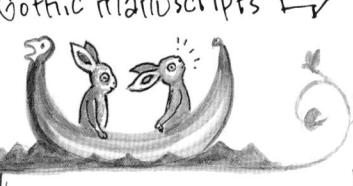

Maybe a third, from the same workshop, but we'll never know. It was buried in a zinc box during World War I where it disintegrated. And so would you.

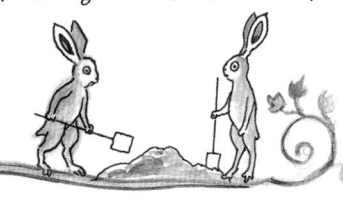

Dad took a fancy to them when he got into his magnum opus, *The History of Humor*.

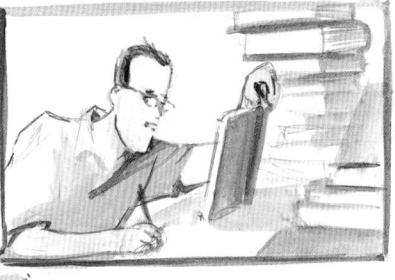

But he got bogged down on that project near the beginning. A Christian bookshop in the U.S.A. decided not to send his internet order for a book that examined occurrences of humor in the holy text of the Bible.

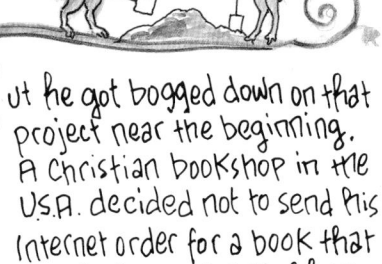

Et must have got onto their shelves by mistake.

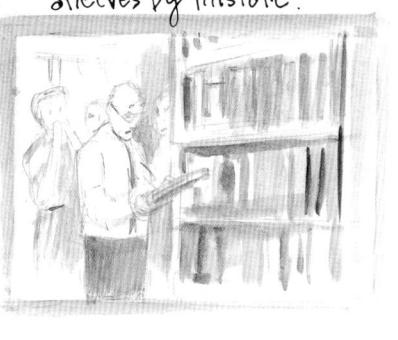

Ike and Mike were like our cats, always doing stuff they weren't supposed to.

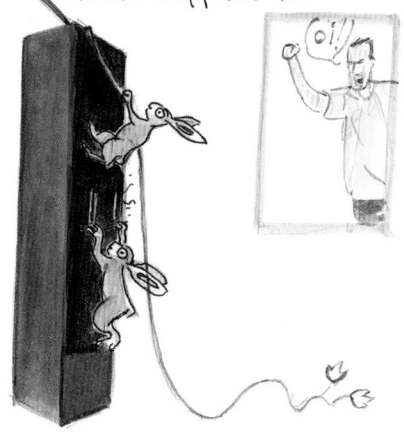

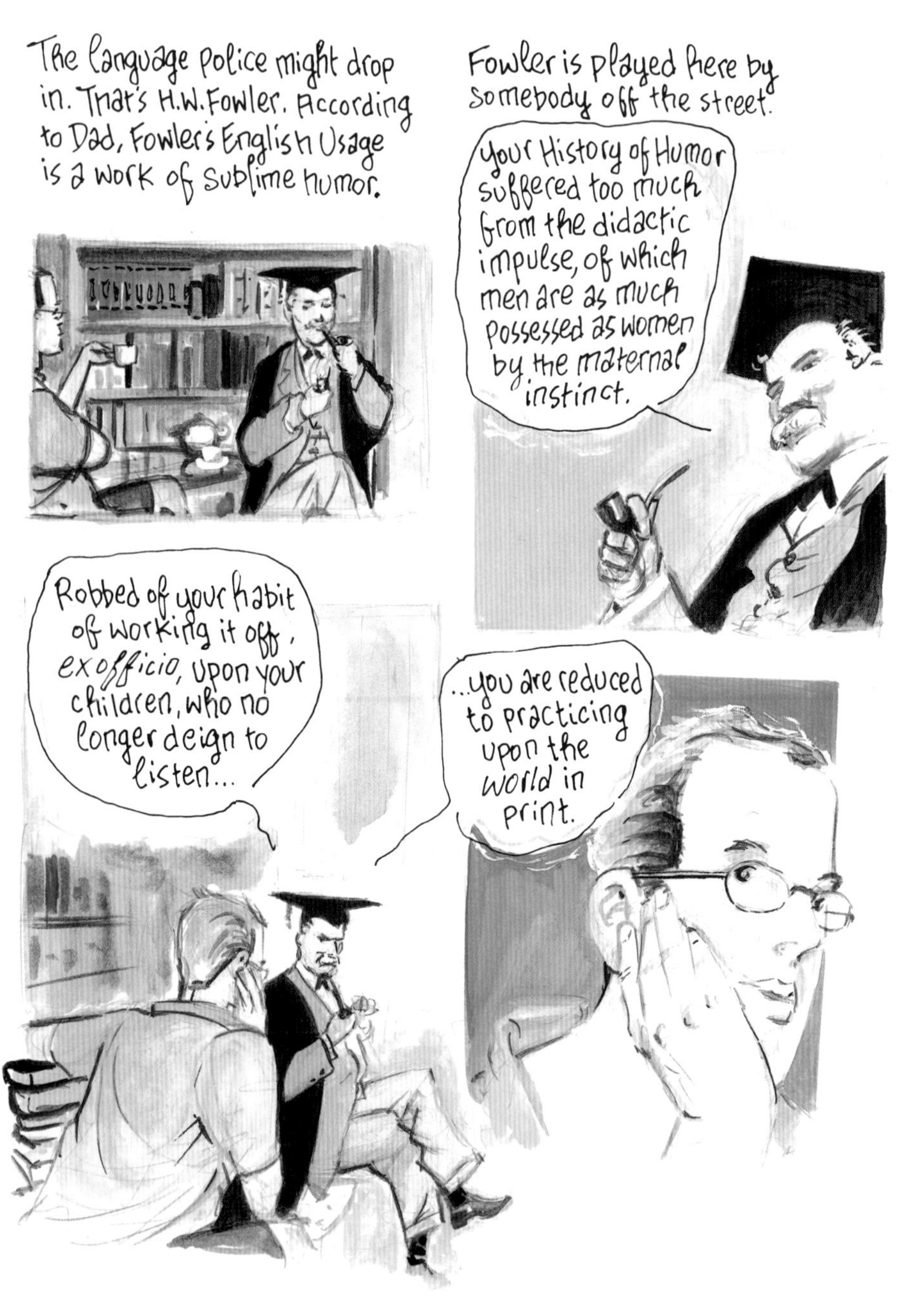
The language police might drop in. That's H.W. Fowler. According to Dad, Fowler's English Usage is a work of sublime humor.
Fowler is played here by somebody off the street.
Your History of Humor suffered too much from the didactic impulse, of which men are as much possessed as women by the maternal instinct.
Robbed of your habit of working it off, ex officio, upon your children, who no longer deign to listen...
...you are reduced to practicing upon the world in print.

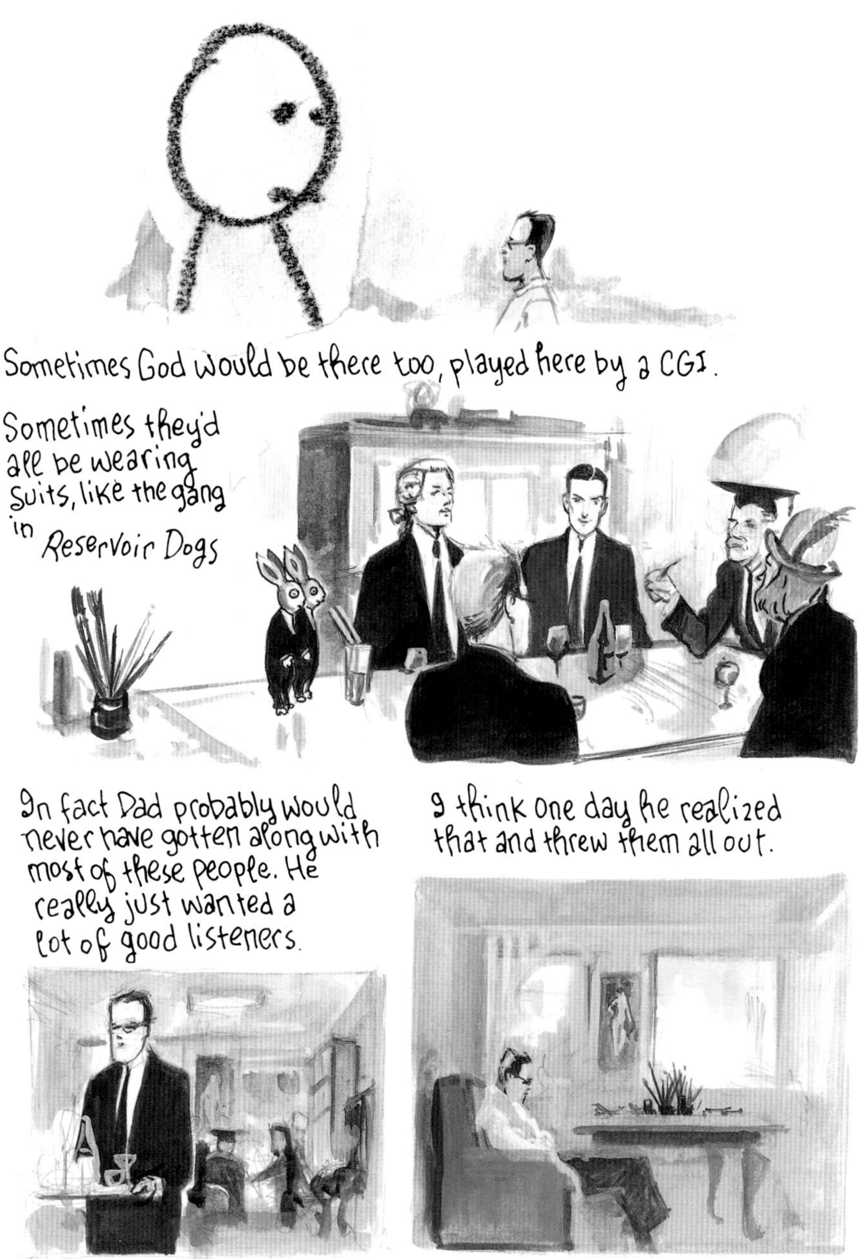
Sometimes God would be there too, played here by a CGI.
Sometimes they'd all be wearing suits, like the gang in Reservoir Dogs
In fact Dad probably would never have gotten along with most of these people. He really just wanted a lot of good listeners.
I think one day he realized that and threw them all out.

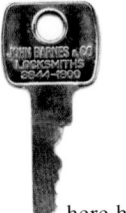

here he is, or was. The artist.

We find his body in the State Reference Library, double-bagged and filed in the deep stack under 741.5, the number recently allotted to graphic novels by the Dewey decimal system.

"I don't get it; how was he able to commit suicide, put himself in two bags, and then seal them with a little metal twisty on the outside?" asks the wife incredulously, the horror of it taking time to sink in.

The librarian runs off to phone the authorities. I leave the wife to handle things. The confusion will give me the time I need to nail the killer.

I find him at home, reading something by A.S. Byatt. "That's the last of your evil designs, Evans."

"So you figured it out. You are a smart fellow, aren't you."

"You have the motive, Evans: revenge. And you're the only one in the picture who knows the Dewey system."

"Yes, well, at least they haven't put all that inferior comic book twaddle near works of true literary merit in the 800s. Campbell's ego was insufferable enough. By the time he got to that last book, *Fate of the Fuckwit* or whatever it's called, he was even insisting on using his own atrocious typesetting."

"He really was nothing, you know. He'd steal my ideas. And in his clumsy way he would rob them of all delight and mirth. He couldn't tell a joke. Nor could he create characters. It was his custom to base them all on friends and family. But I always found myself cast as the characters that met a sticky end. In his *Bacchus* comic he had me sodomized and fed to pigs. In *The Society of Beasts* I was murdered by a raving lunatic wearing a horse's head. And there were others, too dreary to enumerate."

True. I've been through all of Campbell's files.

"When I was told he was going to depict me as an obscure composer named Shobert eating those damn poisonous mushrooms, I could stand the boredom no longer. I had him archived."

It's like the humorous twist ending in one of those 1950s horror comics. Campbell would want to keep a copy.

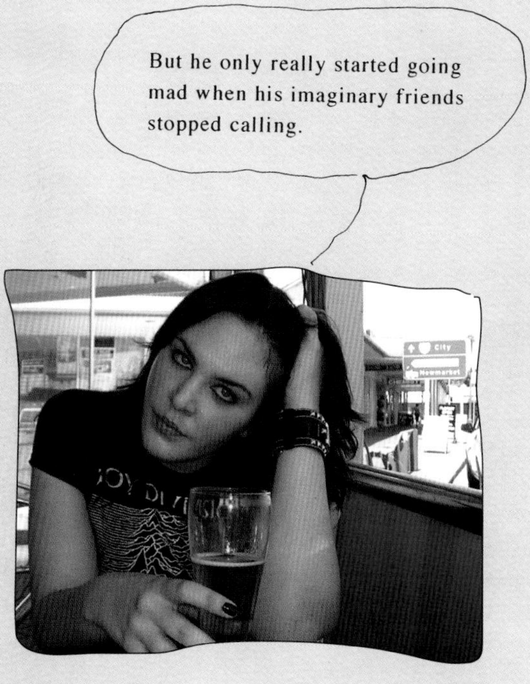
But he only really started going mad when his imaginary friends stopped calling.
City
Newmarket

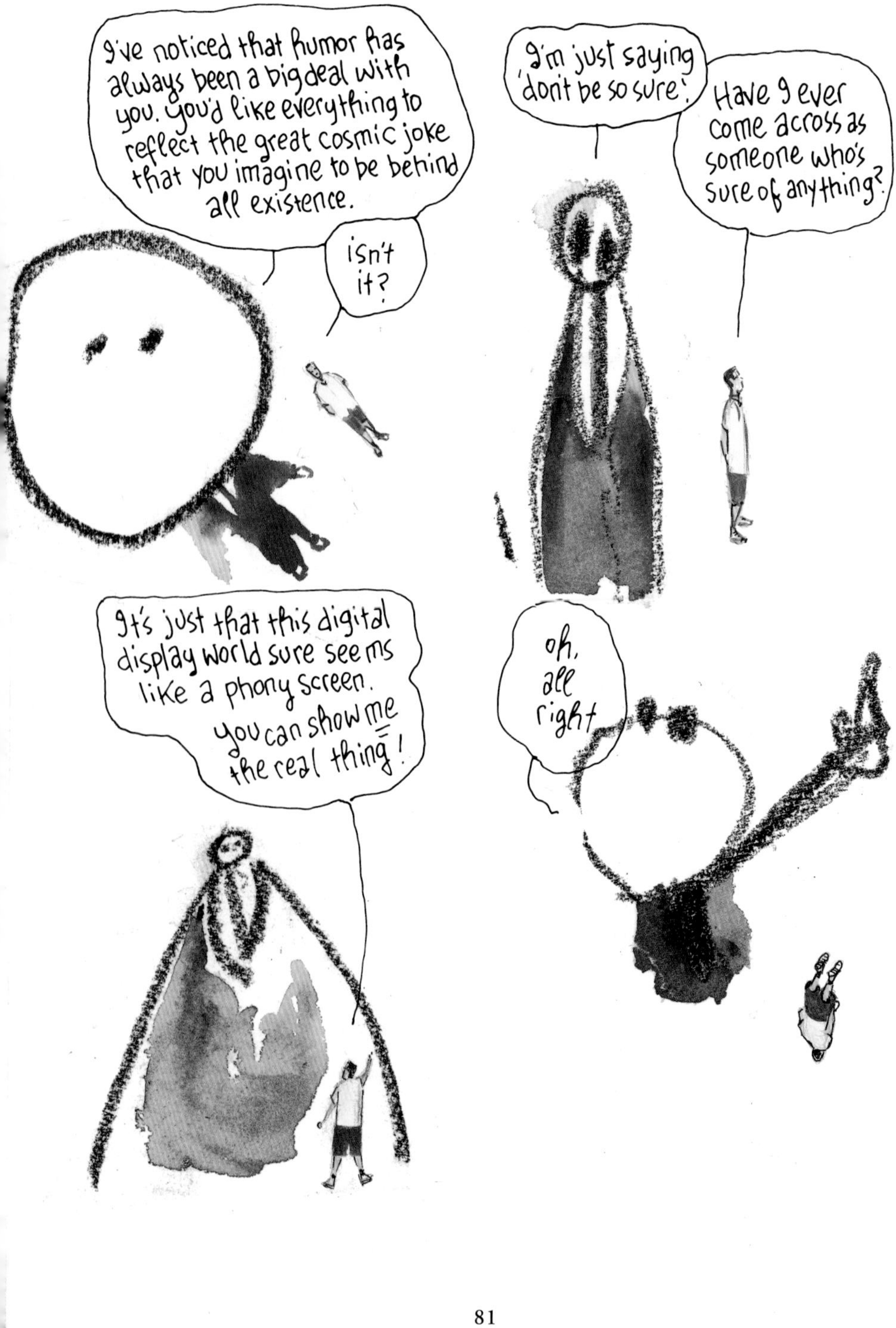
I've noticed that humor has always been a big deal with you. You'd like everything to reflect the great cosmic joke that you imagine to be behind all existence.
isn't it?
I'm just saying 'don't be so sure'.
Have I ever come across as someone who's sure of anything?
It's just that this digital display world sure seems like a phony screen. You can show me the real thing!
oh, all right

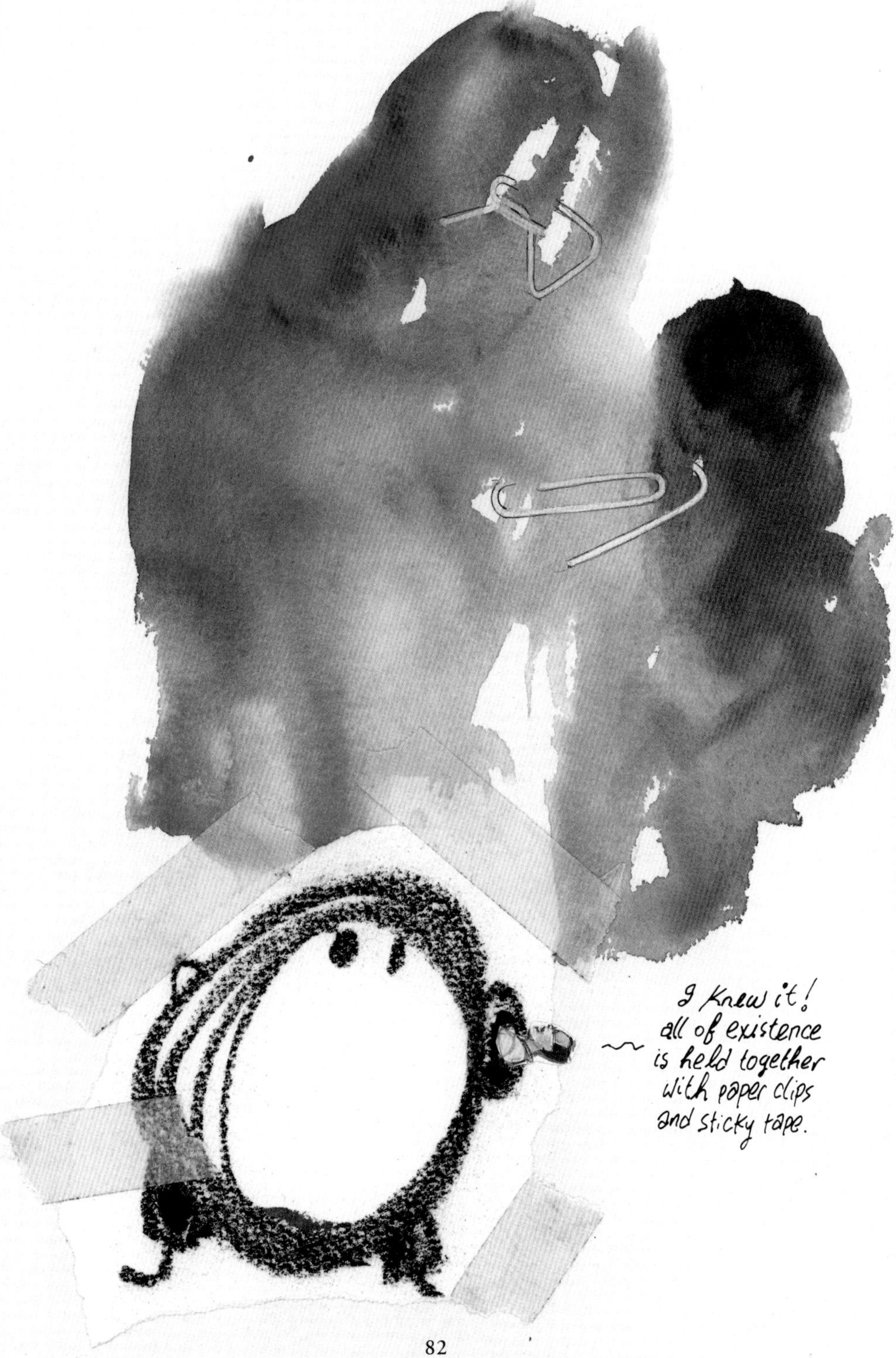
I knew it!
all of existence
is held together
with paper clips
and sticky tape.

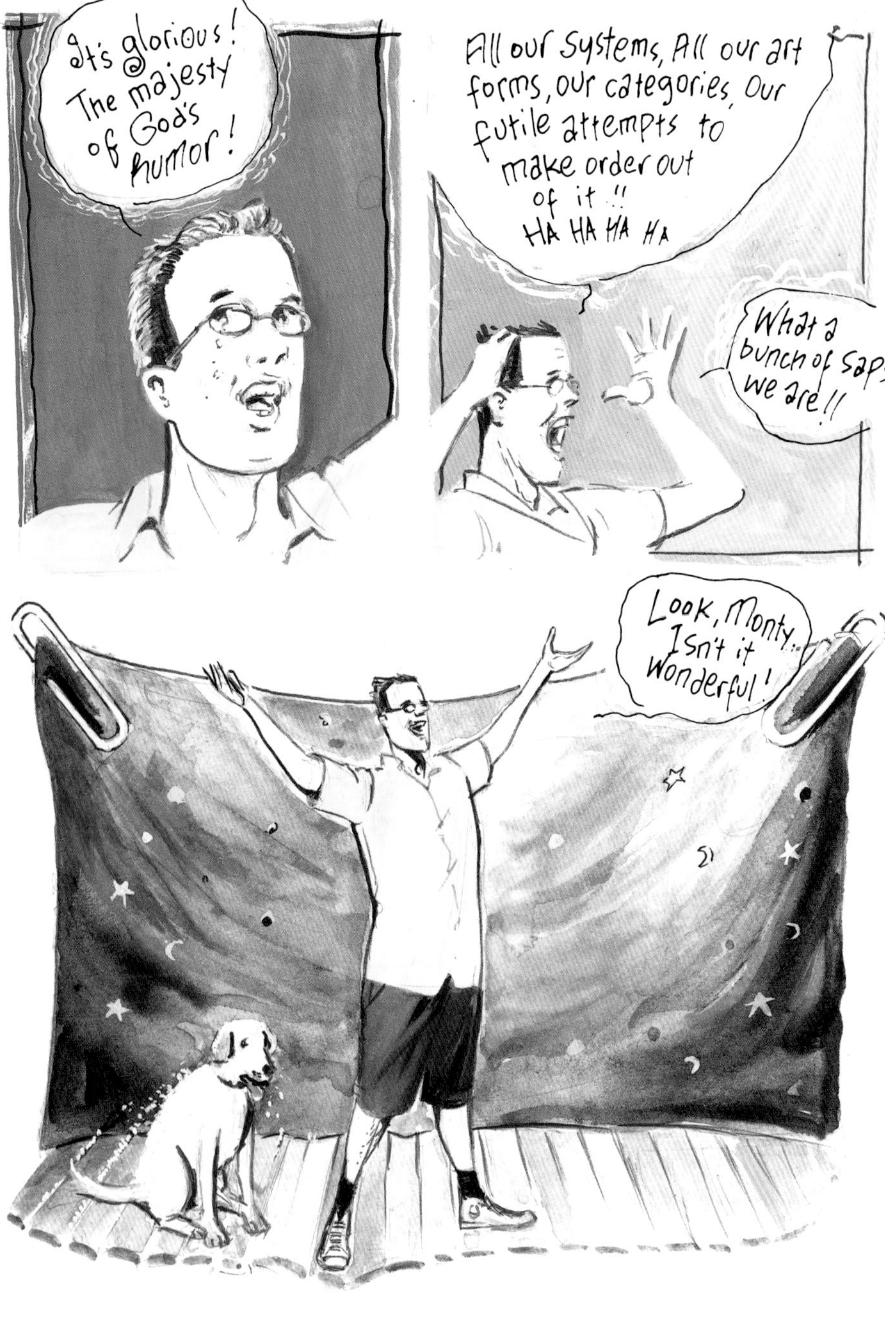
It's glorious! The majesty of God's humor!
All our systems, All our art forms, our categories, our futile attempts to make order out of it!! HA HA HA HA
What a bunch of saps we are!!
Look, Monty... Isn't it wonderful!

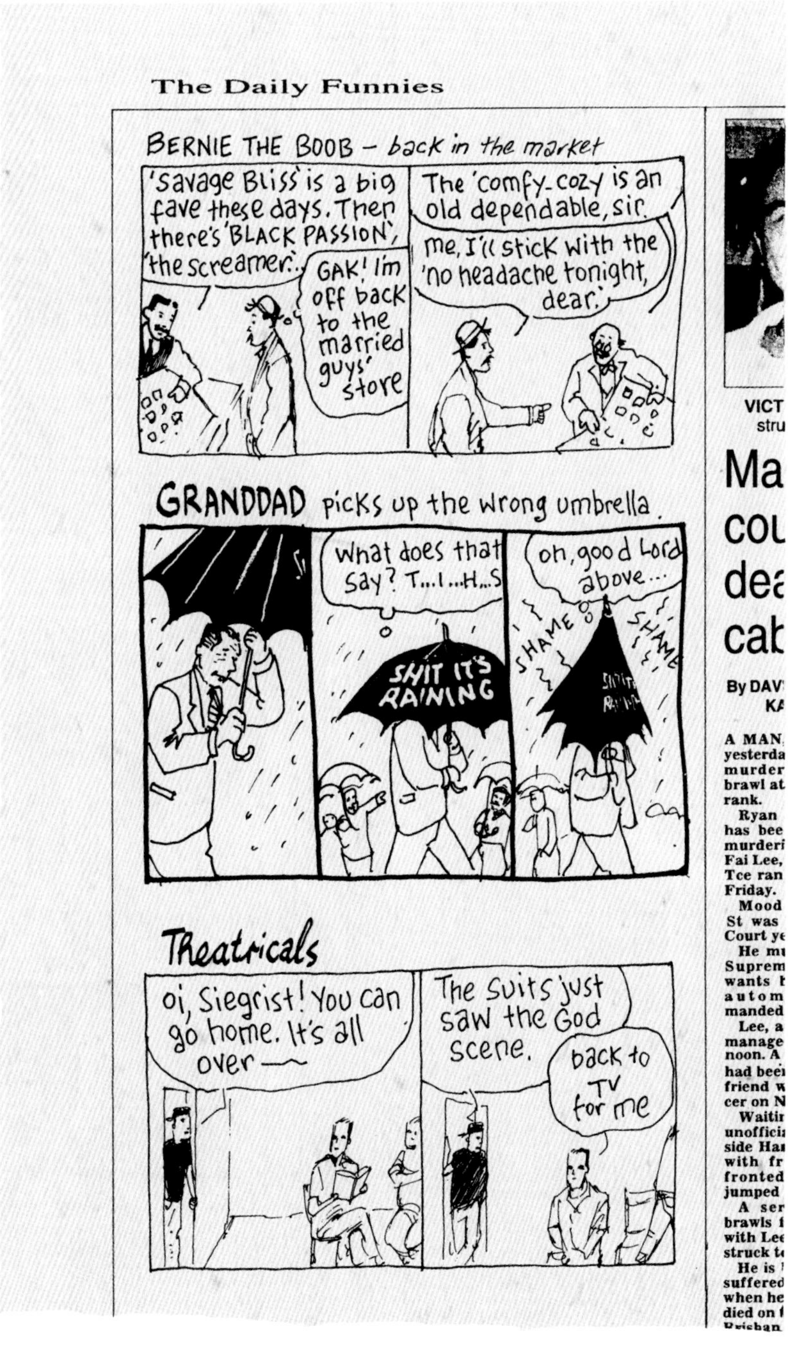
The Daily Funnies
BERNIE THE BOOB – back in the market
'Savage Bliss' is a big fave these days. Then there's 'BLACK PASSION', 'the screamer'..
GAK! I'm off back to the married guys' store
The 'comfy-cozy' is an old dependable, sir.
me, I'll stick with the 'no headache tonight, dear.'
GRANDDAD picks up the wrong umbrella.
What does that say? T...I...H...S
SHIT IT'S RAINING
oh, good Lord above...
SHAME
SHAME
Theatricals
oi, Siegrist! You can go home. It's all over —
The Suits just saw the God scene.
back to TV for me

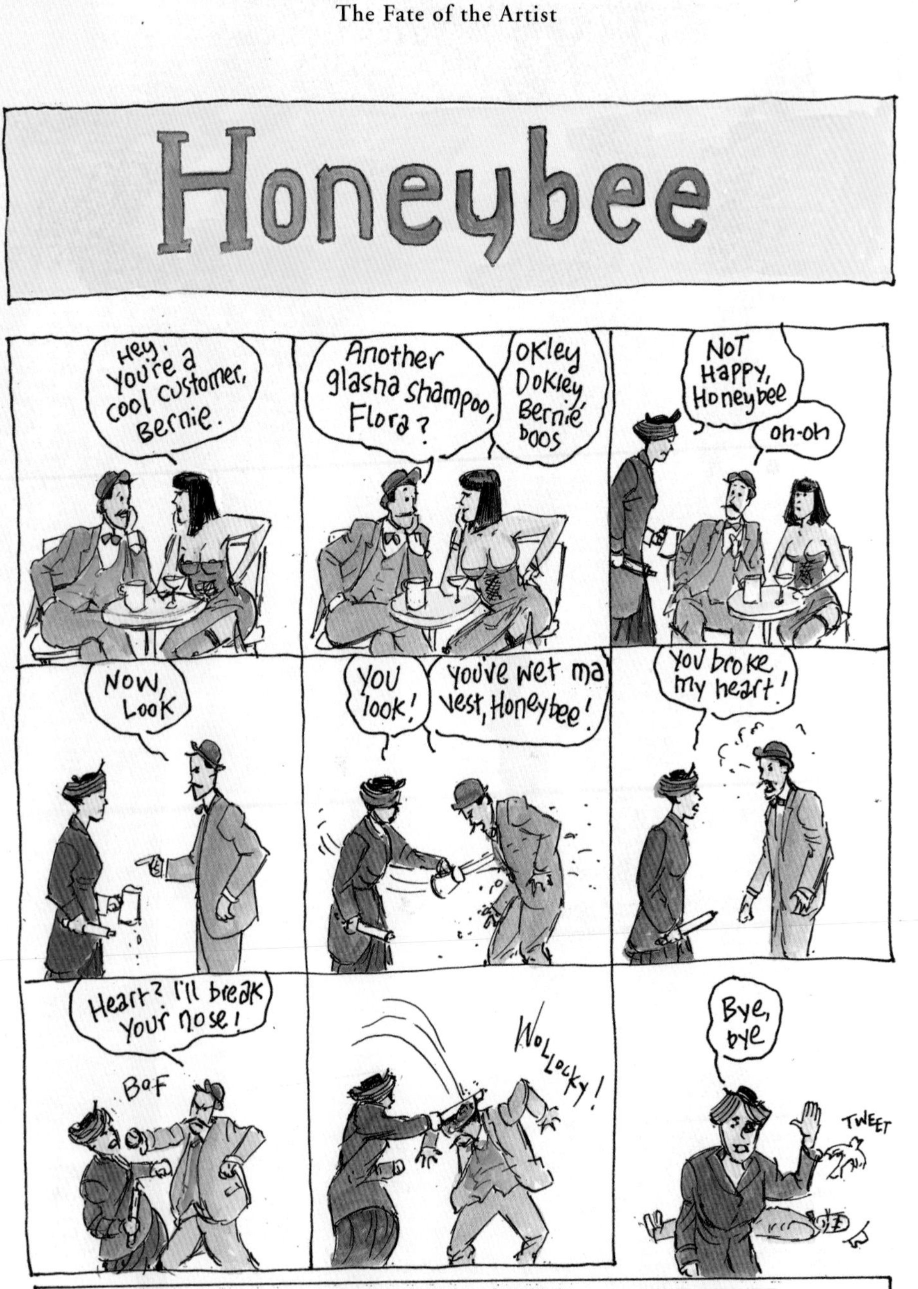
Honeybee
Hey. You're a cool customer, Bernie.
Another glasha shampoo, Flora?
Okley Dokley Bernie boos
Not Happy, Honeybee
oh-oh
Now, Look
You look!
You've wet ma vest, Honeybee!
You broke my heart!
Heart? I'll break your nose!
BoF
WolLocky!
Bye, bye
TWEET
LOOK FOR HONEYBEE EVERY MONTH IN LAFF-A-MINUTE.

Page 4

In the following dramatization
of the short story by O.Henry,

THE
CONFESSIONS
OF
A HUMORIST,

the leading role is played by

Mr. Eddie Campbell.

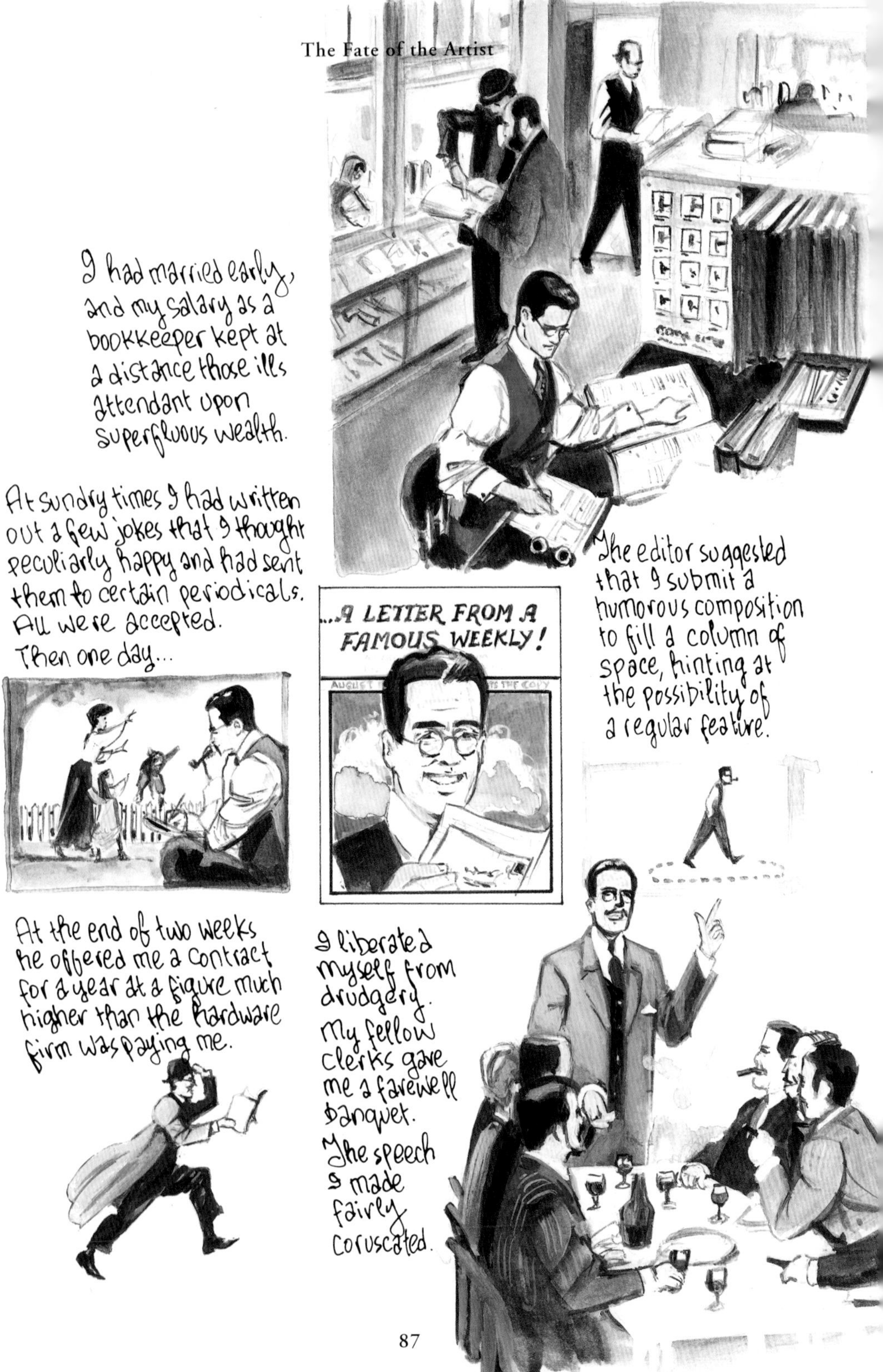
I had married early, and my salary as a bookkeeper kept at a distance those ills attendant upon superfluous wealth.
At sundry times I had written out a few jokes that I thought peculiarly happy and had sent them to certain periodicals. All were accepted.
Then one day...
...A LETTER FROM A FAMOUS WEEKLY!
The editor suggested that I submit a humorous composition to fill a column of space, hinting at the possibility of a regular feature.
At the end of two weeks he offered me a contract for a year at a figure much higher than the hardware firm was paying me.
I liberated myself from drudgery.
My fellow clerks gave me a farewell banquet.
The speech I made fairly coruscated.

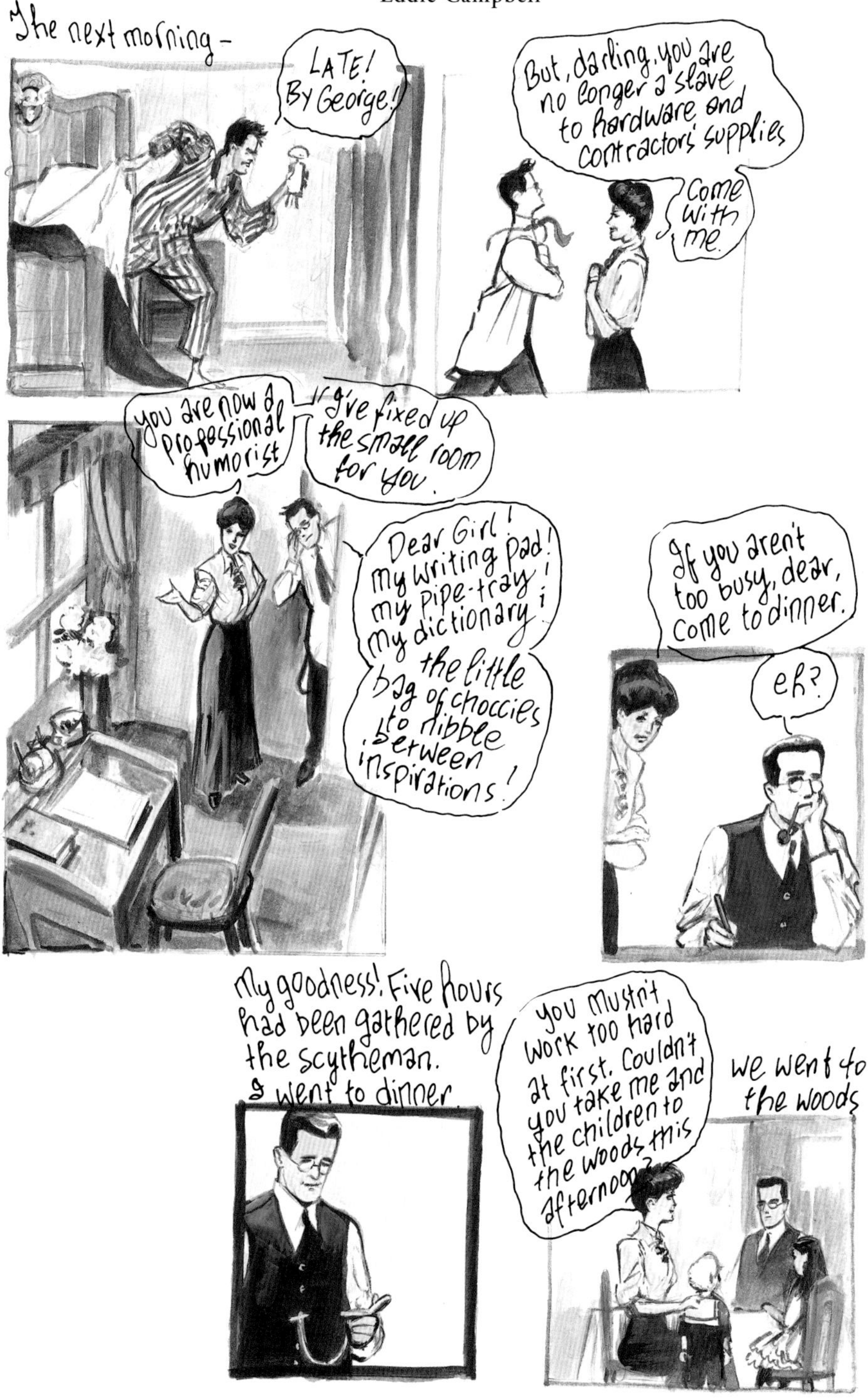
The next morning -
LATE! By George!
But, darling, you are no longer a slave to hardware and contractors' supplies
Come with me.
You are now a professional humorist
I've fixed up the small room for you.
Dear Girl! my writing pad! my pipe-tray! my dictionary!
the little bag of choccies to nibble between inspirations!
If you aren't too busy, dear, come to dinner.
eh?
My goodness! Five hours had been gathered by the scytheman.
I went to dinner.
You mustn't work too hard at first. Couldn't you take me and the children to the woods this afternoon?
We went to the woods.

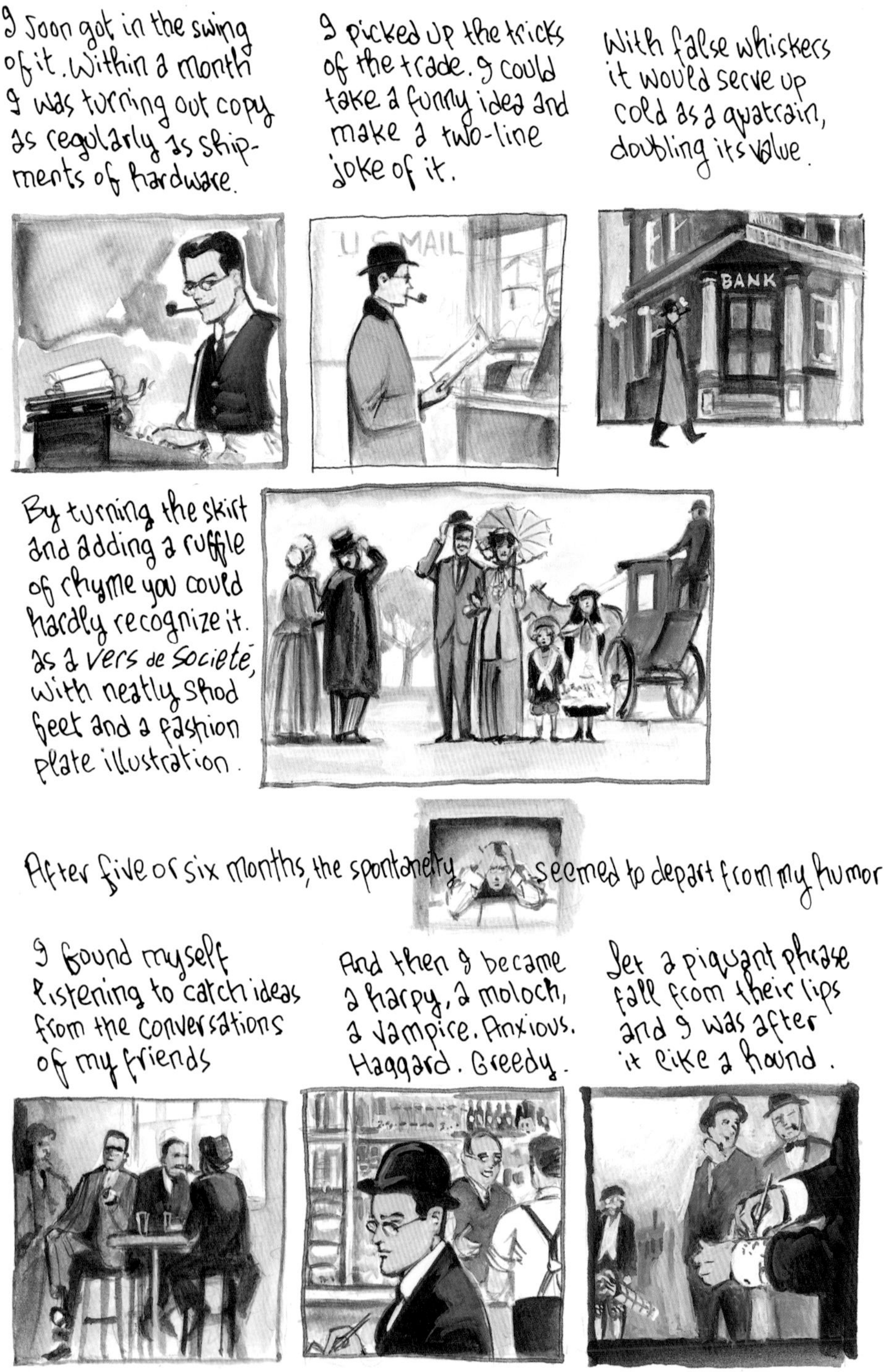
I soon got in the swing of it. Within a month I was turning out copy as regularly as shipments of hardware.
I picked up the tricks of the trade. I could take a funny idea and make a two-line joke of it.
U.S. MAIL
With false whiskers it would serve up cold as a quatrain, doubling its value.
BANK
By turning the skirt and adding a ruffle of rhyme you could hardly recognize it. as a vers de société, with neatly shod feet and a fashion plate illustration.
After five or six months, the spontaneity seemed to depart from my humor
I found myself listening to catch ideas from the conversations of my friends
And then I became a harpy, a moloch, a vampire. Anxious. Haggard. Greedy.
Let a piquant phrase fall from their lips and I was after it like a hound.

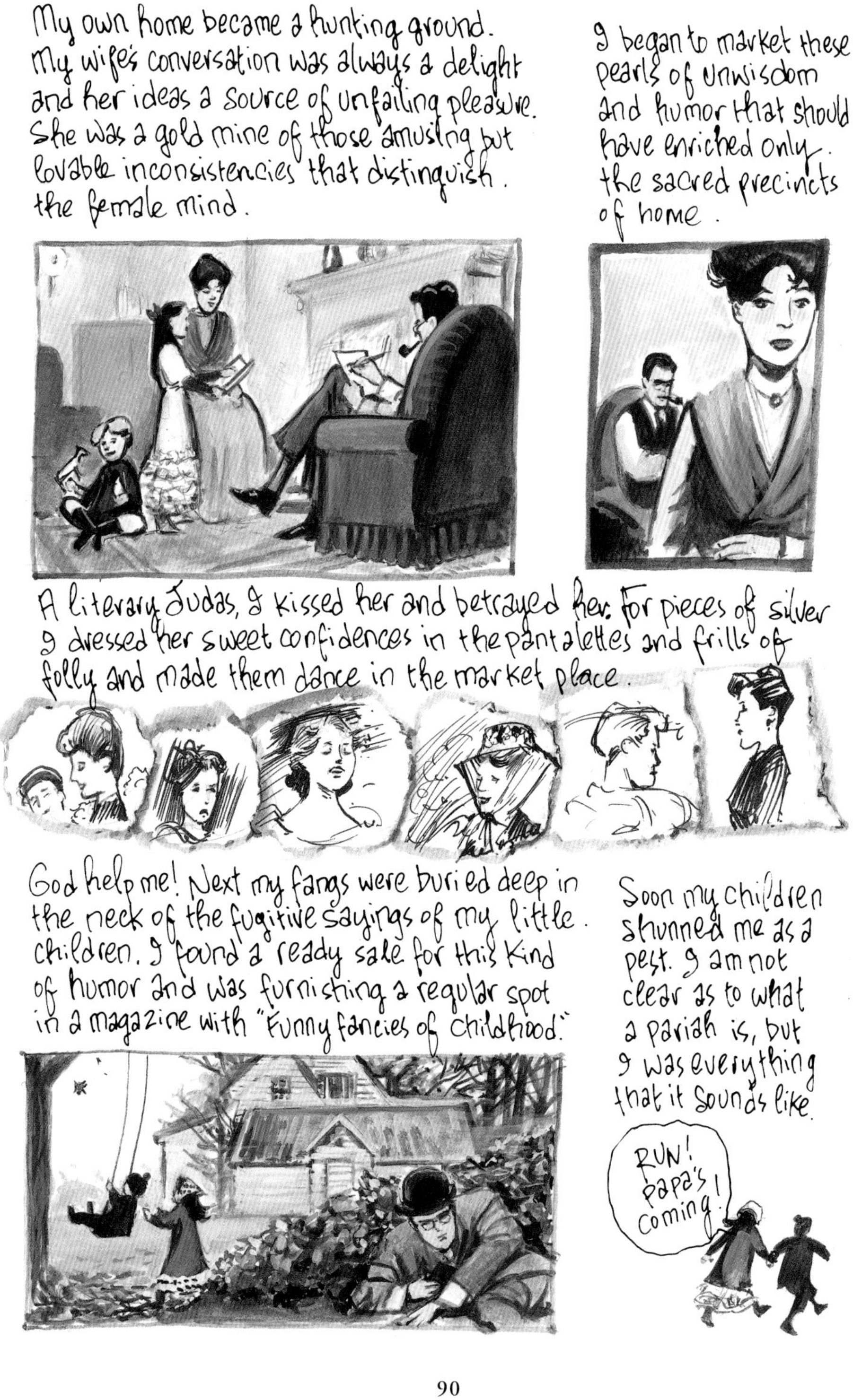
My own home became a hunting ground. My wife's conversation was always a delight and her ideas a source of unfailing pleasure. She was a gold mine of those amusing but lovable inconsistencies that distinguish the female mind.
I began to market these pearls of unwisdom and humor that should have enriched only the sacred precincts of home.
A literary Judas, I kissed her and betrayed her. For pieces of silver I dressed her sweet confidences in the pantalettes and frills of folly and made them dance in the market place.
God help me! Next my fangs were buried deep in the neck of the fugitive sayings of my little children. I found a ready sale for this kind of humor and was furnishing a regular spot in a magazine with "Funny fancies of childhood."
Soon my children shunned me as a pest. I am not clear as to what a pariah is, but I was everything that it sounds like.
RUN! Papa's coming!

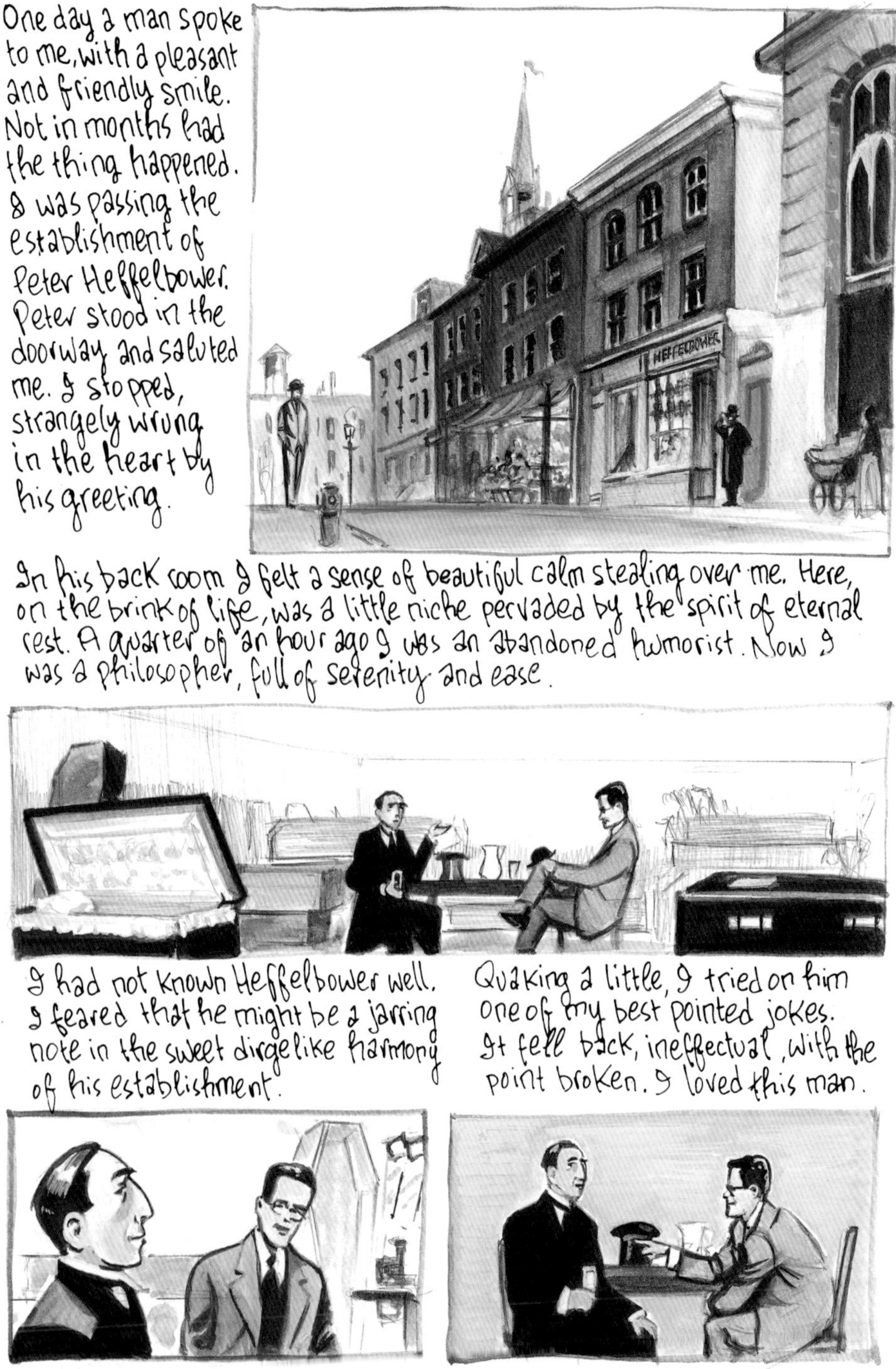
One day a man spoke to me, with a pleasant and friendly smile. Not in months had the thing happened. I was passing the establishment of Peter Heffelbower. Peter stood in the doorway and saluted me. I stopped, strangely wrung in the heart by his greeting.
HEFFELBOWER
In his back room I felt a sense of beautiful calm stealing over me. Here, on the brink of life, was a little niche pervaded by the spirit of eternal rest. A quarter of an hour ago I was an abandoned humorist. Now I was a philosopher, full of serenity and ease.
I had not known Heffelbower well. I feared that he might be a jarring note in the sweet dirgelike harmony of his establishment.
Quaking a little, I tried on him one of my best pointed jokes. It fell back, ineffectual, with the point broken. I loved this man.

Two or three evenings each week I would steal down to Heffelbower's and revel in his back room. In no other place could I throw off my habit of extracting humorous ideas from my surroundings.

My work began to suffer. It was not the pain and burden to me that it had been. I worked impatiently, anxious to be off to my helpful retreat as a drunkard is to get to his tavern.

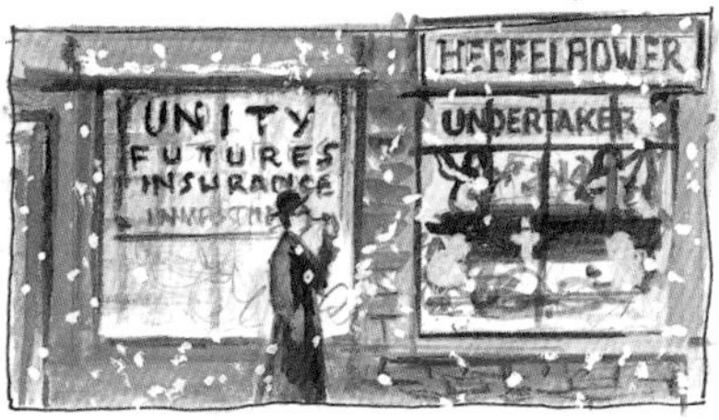
HEFFELBOWER
UNDERTAKER
UNITY
FUTURES
INSURANCE

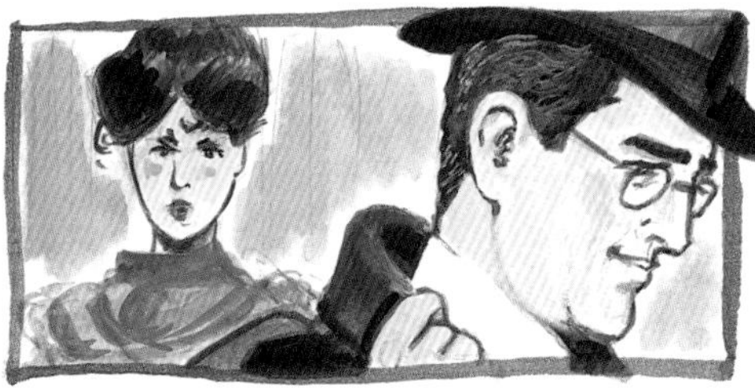

One day I brought home a silver coffin handle for a paperweight and a fine, fluffy hearse plume to dust my papers with. But Louisa found them and shrieked with horror.

Heffelbower laid before me a temptation that swept me off my feet. In his sensible, uninspired way, he showed me his books and explained that his profits were increasing rapidly.

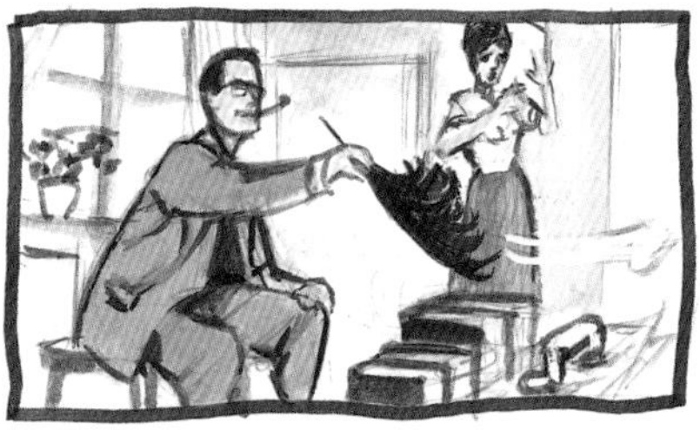

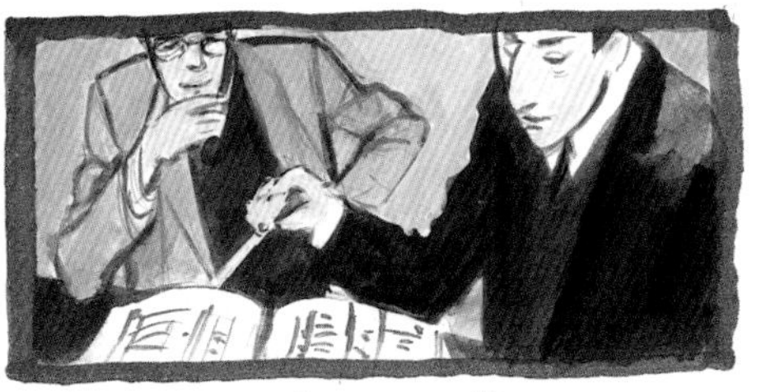

He had thought of taking on a partner with some cash. When I left his place he had my check for the thousand I had in the bank.

I was dreading to tell Louisa about it. But I walked on air. To once more enjoy the apples of life instead of squeezing them to a pulp for a few drops of hard cider to make the public feel funny.

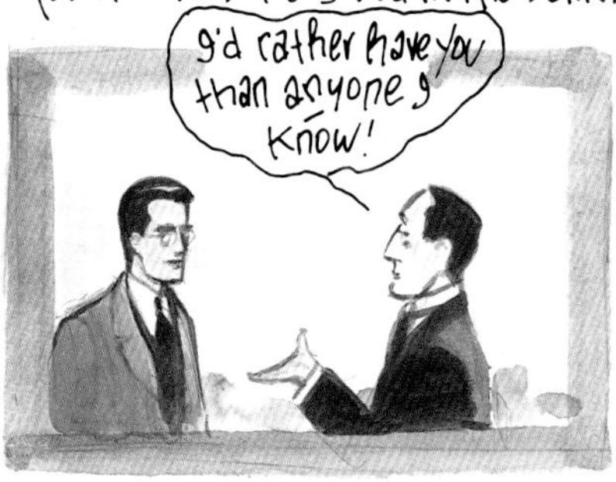
I'd rather have you than anyone I know!

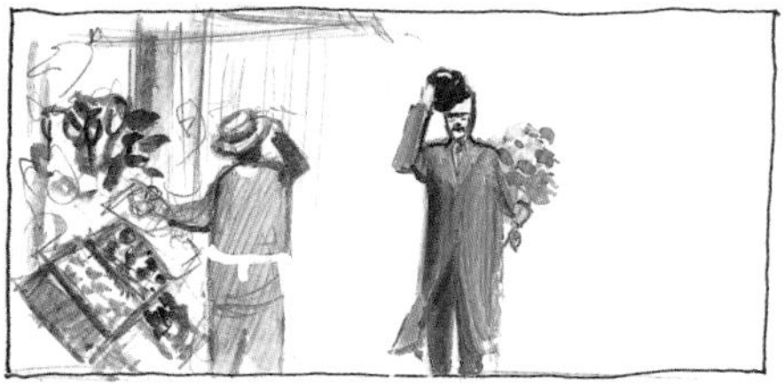

At supper Louisa handed me some letters with rejected manuscripts. Since I began going to Heffelbower's my stuff had been coming back with alarming frequency.

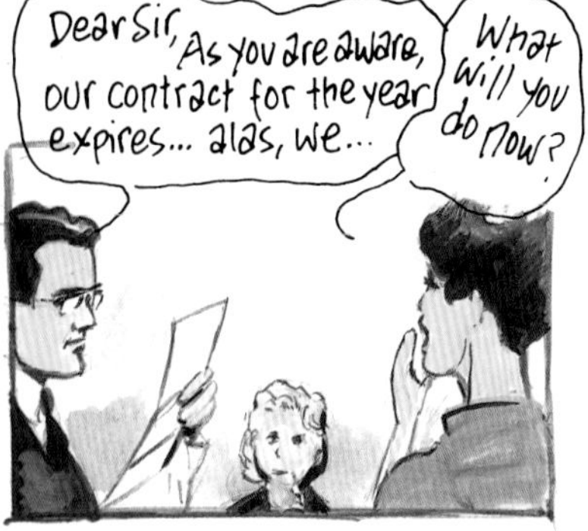
Dear Sir, As you are aware, our contract for the year expires... alas, we...
What will you do now?

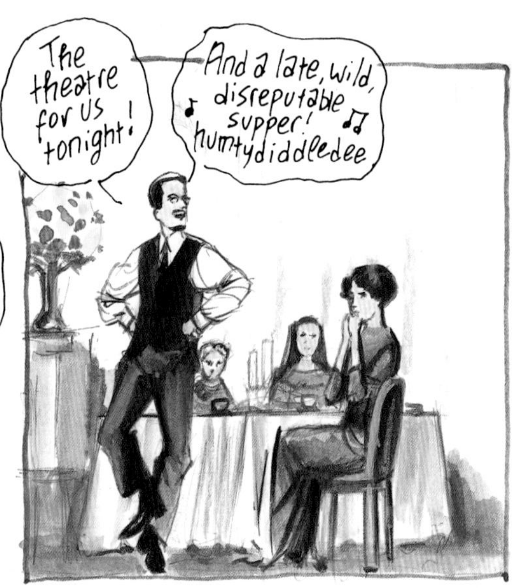
The theatre for us tonight!
And a late, wild, disreputable supper! humtydiddledee

In conclusion I will say that you will find no man in our town as well liked, as jovial and full of merry sayings as I. Once more I take pleasure in Louisa's confidential chatter without a mercenary thought, while Guy and Viola play at my feet, distributing gems of childish humor without fear of the ghastly tormentor who used to dog their steps, notebook in hand.

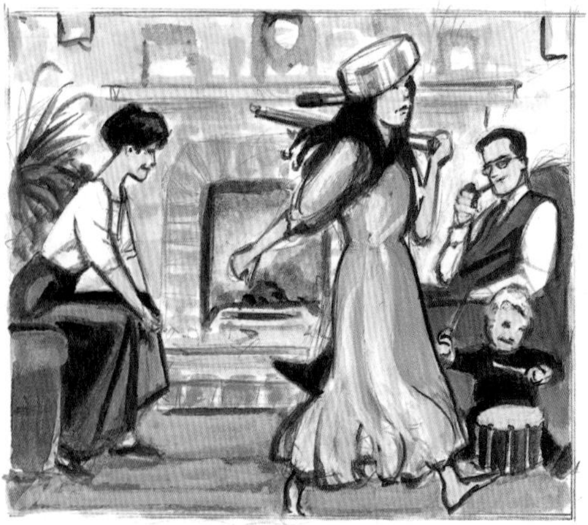

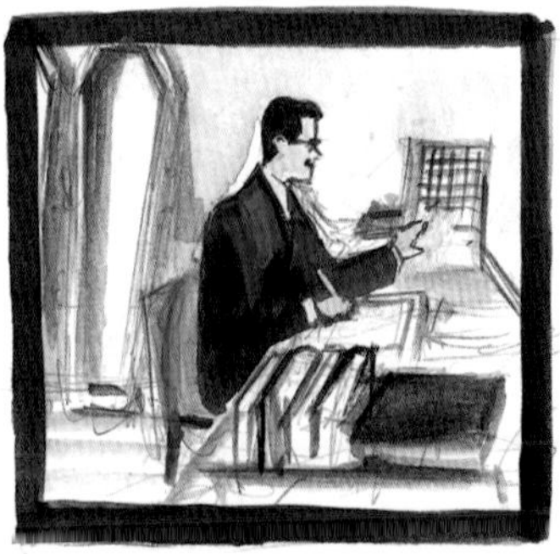

Our business has prospered. I keep the books and look after the shop while Peter attends to outside matters. He says that my levity would simply turn any funeral into a regular Irish wake.

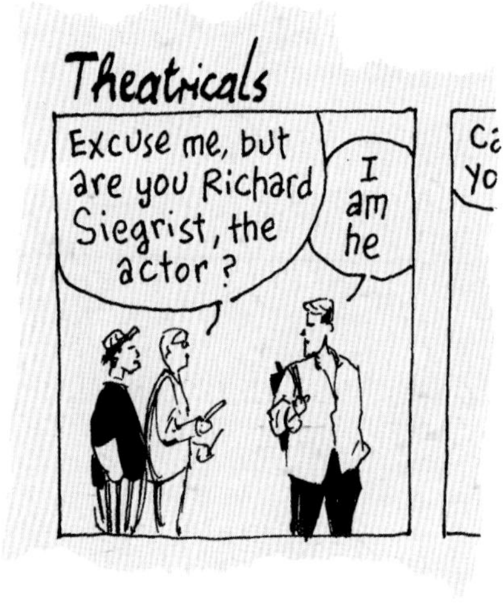
Theatricals
Excuse me, but are you Richard Siegrist, the actor?
I am he

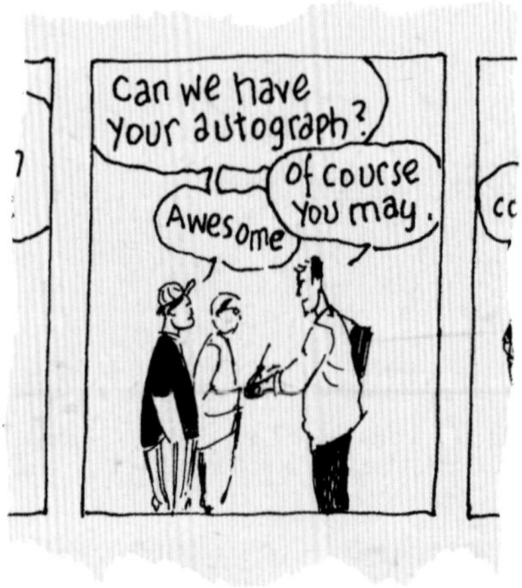
Can we have your autograph?
Of course you may.
Awesome

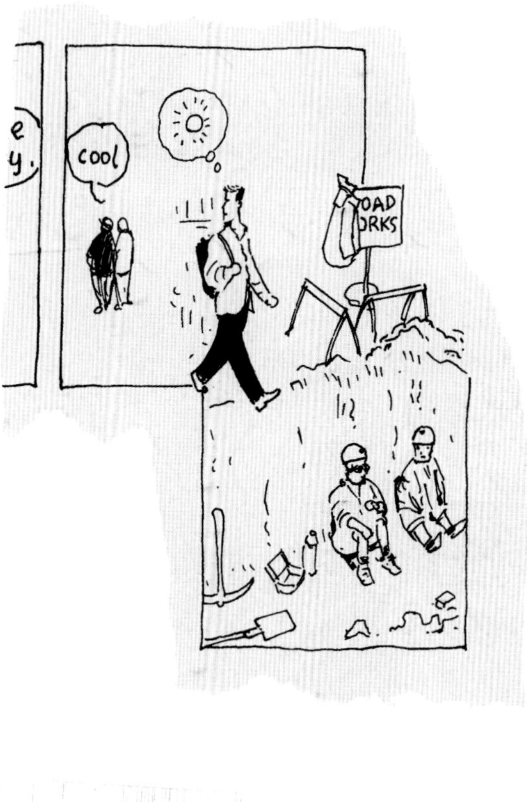
cool